Issues in Focus

The American Civil Rights Movement
The African-American Struggle for Equality

Linda Jacobs Altman

Enslow Publishers, Inc.

40 Industrial Road   PO Box 38
Box 398   Aldershot
Berkeley Heights, NJ 07922   Hants GU12 6BP
USA   UK

http://www.enslow.com

Library of Congress Cataloging-in-Publication Data

Altman, Linda Jacobs, 1943-
   The American civil rights movement : the African-American struggle for equality / Linda Jacobs Altman.
      v. cm. — (Issues in focus)
   Includes bibliographical references and index.
   Contents: Slavery and reconstruction—Beginnings of the movement—Challenging Jim Crow segregation—Montgomery, Alabama: the bus boycott—Pioneers in school integration—The beginnings of sixties activism—Activism in the deep South—"We shall overcome": the movement expands—The turn to militance.
   ISBN 0-7660-1944-6 (hardcover : alk. paper)
      1. African Americans—Civil rights—History—20th century—Juvenile literature. 2. Civil rights movements—United States—History—20th century—Juvenile literature. 3. United States—Race relations—Juvenile literature. [1. African Americans—Civil rights—History—20th century. 2. Civil rights movements. 3. Race relations.] I. Title. II. Issues in focus (Hillside, N.J.)
   E185.61.A447 2004
   323.1196'073—dc22
                                                    2003018171

Printed in the United States of America

10 9 8 7 6 5 4 3 2 1

To Our Readers: We have done our best to make sure all Internet Addresses in this book were active and appropriate when we went to press. However, the author and the publisher have no control over and assume no liability for the material available on those Internet sites or on links to other Web sites. Any comments or suggestions can be sent by e-mail to comments@enslow.com or to the address on the back cover.

Every effort has been made to locate all copyright holders of material used in this book. If any errors or omissions have occurred, corrections will be made in future editions of this book.

Illustration Credits: AP/Wide World, pp. 46, 61, 67, 83, 92, 94; © Bettman/Corbis, p. 86; courtesy of the Birmingham Public Library Department of Archives and Manuscripts (Catalog No. 1125.11.20 A-1), p. 51; Will Counts, p. 57; © Hulton-Deutsch Collection/Corbis, p. 37; Library of Congress, pp. 7, 14, 20, 24, 29, 34, 40, 72, 77, 100, 110; Mississippi Department of Archives and History, p. 103.

Cover Illustration: All photos are from the Library of Congress except for those from the Mississippi Department of Archives and History (lower right corner) and the National Archives (upper right corner).

Contents

1

Slavery and Reconstruction

On July 25, 1974, African-American Congresswoman Barbara Jordan of Texas stood before the House of Representatives. She talked about the opening words of the U.S. Constitution: *We the people . . .*

It's a very eloquent beginning. But when that document was completed on the seventeenth of September in 1787, I was not included in that *We the people*. I felt somehow for many years that George Washington and Alexander Hamilton just left me out by mistake. But through the process of amendment, interpretation, and court decisions, I have finally been included in *We the people*.[1]

The story of the civil rights movement is the story of how African Americans in the United States won the right to be included. It was a long, hard struggle.

Africans came to this country as cargo. White people bought and sold them like livestock. To justify this, slave owners claimed that black people were inferior to whites. Some said that blacks were born for service. Some said that they were little more than animals in human form.

The emancipation, or freeing, of the slaves did not change these racist ideas. The white ruling class developed laws, rules, and policies to keep African Americans "in their place."

Even abolitionists, people who wanted to end slavery, did not necessarily accept African Americans as equals. Many believed that whites were superior to blacks. They simply did not agree that anyone should hold another human being as property.

Abraham Lincoln himself, often called the "great emancipator" because he freed the slaves, once stated that he did not believe in racial equality:

> I am not . . . in favor of bringing about in any way the social and political equality of the white and black races. . . . I am not . . . in favor of making voters or jurors of negroes, nor of qualifying them to hold office, nor to intermarry with white people; and I [believe that] there is a physical difference between the white and black races which . . . will [prevent them from] living together [as equals]. . . . while they do remain together there must be the position of superior and inferior, and I am in favor of having the superior position [given] to the white race."[2]

For nearly four hundred years, slaves were transported to the Americas from Africa. Chained up in the dark, without adequate food, water, or fresh air, thousands of the captives died.

At the beginning of the Civil War, Lincoln cared more about preserving the Union than freeing the slaves. Many of the men who fought for that Union shared his beliefs. Even after the Emancipation Proclamation of January 1, 1863, "freedom" did not mean "equality." For that, African Americans had a long way to go.

Reconstruction and the Black Codes

After the Civil War, the government began a program of Reconstruction in the South. It aimed to rebuild the former Confederacy and help freed slaves adjust to their new lives.

The U.S. Congress passed three new constitutional amendments that directly affected African Americans. The Thirteenth Amendment, which was ratified, or approved, on December 6, 1865, outlawed slavery everywhere in the United States. The Fourteenth Amendment, ratified on July 28, 1868, gave African Americans the rights of U.S. citizenship, and the Fifteenth Amendment, ratified on February 3, 1870, specifically protected their voting rights.

A federal agency called the Freedmen's Bureau provided financial aid, educational programs, and social services for freed slaves. White southerners tried to counteract these reforms with "Black Codes." These codes were state and local laws that, among other things, set curfews for African Americans, required them to have a "pass" to enter certain areas, or limited them to employment as field hands and household servants.

Reconstruction officials soon recognized the Black Codes for what they were: attempts to get around the law and reduce African Americans to a condition as near to slavery as possible. The federal government suspended the codes.

Through the years of Reconstruction, African-American people began to vote and to run for elective office. Louisiana elected the first black governor in U.S. history, P.B.S. Pinchback. Mississippi sent two African-American men, Blanche K. Bruce and Hiram Revels, to the United States Senate.

The Freedmen's Bureau built more than four

thousand educational institutions, from elementary schools to colleges such as Howard University in Washington, D.C. Former slaves who had been kept illiterate and ignorant by their owners now sent their children to school and often went themselves. To them, education was a precious reward of freedom. They wanted to read, to write, to make up for lost time.

Plessy v. *Ferguson*

Reconstruction ended in 1877, when President Rutherford B. Hayes pulled out the last of the federal troops. This left white southerners free to reverse African-American gains. The whites found unexpected help from three Supreme Court decisions.

The Court struck down the Civil Rights Act of 1875, which protected rights "to the full and equal enjoyment of the accommodations, advantages, facilities, and privileges of inns, public [transportation] . . . theaters, and other places of public amusement."[3]

In another ruling, the Court limited Fourteenth Amendment protections against discrimination. The justices ruled that the amendment applied only to public, or government, organizations and facilities. Individuals and private organizations could exclude African Americans without penalty.

In 1896, the landmark case of *Plessy* v. *Ferguson* finished what these other rulings had started. On June 7, 1892, Louisiana carpenter Homer Plessy boarded a train and sat in a car set aside for whites only. The authorities arrested him under an 1890 state law that separated the races on public transportation.

The *Plessy* case went all the way to the Supreme Court. The Court ruled that racial separation did not violate African-American rights, so long as facilities for blacks were equal to those for whites. Thus, *Plessy* v. *Ferguson* laid the legal foundation for the "separate but equal" doctrine. This doctrine in turn became the foundation for the strict segregation policies known as "Jim Crow" laws.

The Beginnings of "Jim Crow"

Jim Crow was a minstrel show character—a bumbling fool played by a white performer in "blackface" makeup. No one seems to know just how the name became associated with segregation laws. But by the turn of the twentieth century, Americans understood that "Jim Crow" meant laws that separated the races.

These state laws started with the old Black Codes and then went far beyond them. In painstaking detail they created two separate and unequal worlds. Blacks and whites could not go to the same schools, eat in the same restaurants, or use the same public restrooms or water fountains. In some states, they could not even be buried in the same cemeteries.

To survive in a Jim Crow world, African Americans had to obey not only the written laws, but the unwritten ones as well. Basically, this meant living according to white expectations. African Americans had to appear ignorant, impoverished, and servile.

For example, African Americans who made good money dared not "show off" with nice clothes, late model cars, or beautiful homes. Some people found clever ways around these unwritten rules. They fixed up the inside of their homes, but made the outside look like a tumbledown shanty. They would leave their houses unpainted, scatter junk all over the yard, and generally try to "look poor."

Most important of all, black people had to be respectful to whites. Former sharecropper Edgar Williams explained:

> As far as the white man was concerned you were never to call him by his name. You always said "Mr." or "Mrs." or "Boss," or "Captain." We were very much in danger because we had to do what the white man told us to do. If we didn't then they would get together and beat you up.[4]

Jim Crow put African Americans in a no-win situation. To advance themselves in life, black people had to move beyond the old stereotypes. To survive in a world ruled by whites, they had to behave as if those stereotypes were true.

Black people in the Jim Crow South had to show by every word and gesture that they "knew their place." Whites expected African Americans to hang their heads, grinning and mumbling and generally behaving as if they could not understand the simplest instructions.

African-American parents explained these facts to their children. Blues musician Willie Thomas remembered what his father once told him: "Honor the white folks, honor 'em, yassuh an' nosuh. You have to do that."[5]

The closest most black people came to any title of

respect from whites was "Uncle" or "Aunty" so-and-so. Otherwise, whites called them by their first names only, ignoring last names and titles such as doctor, reverend, and even Mr., Mrs., or Miss. African-American men learned to answer to "boy" regardless of their age or position in life.

Booker T. Washington and Tuskegee Institute

Booker T. Washington was born a slave in Virginia, sometime in 1856 or 1857. He never knew his father or the date of his own birth. He did not have a last name until years later, when he took "Washington" in tribute to the first president.

More than anything, Washington wanted to go to school, but he could not. There was a law against educating slaves, and the ruling class took that law seriously. Not until emancipation could this child with no history fulfill the dream of his young life. He learned to read and write and also to cope in the world beyond the backcountry farm where he was born.

At the age of sixteen, Washington enrolled in the Hampton Institute, a private school for African-American students. He later became a teacher there.

Working at the Hampton Institute convinced Washington that vocational training would help freed slaves more than an academic education. Academics prepared students to become doctors, lawyers, teachers, and other professionals. Vocational education prepared them to become carpenters, printers, bricklayers, and shoemakers. Trades such as these, Washington reasoned, would prepare students for jobs they could reasonably hope to obtain. This would give them an economic foundation for improving their lot in life.

In 1881, Washington founded the Tuskegee Normal and Industrial Institute in Alabama, to give young African Americans a quality vocational education. The school later shortened its name to Tuskegee Institute; it is now Tuskegee University.

Washington hoped that the prospect of a productive black working class that knew its "place" would appeal to southern whites. In large measure Washington's plan did appeal to whites, mostly because Booker T. Washington limited his goals. He did not challenge Jim Crow laws or demand voting rights for African Americans. He was willing to put off political and social equality indefinitely in order to improve economic opportunities for his people.

In 1895, in a speech that came to be known as the Atlanta Compromise, he made his position clear. He told African Americans to accept the limitations placed upon them and work within the system: "The masses of us are to live by the productions of our hands. . . . we shall prosper . . . as we learn to dignify and glorify common labor, and put brains and skill into the common occupations of life."[6]

He reassured whites that "in all things that are purely social [blacks and whites] can be as separate as the fingers, yet one as the hand in all things essential to mutual progress." For African Americans just coming out of slavery, he said, "the opportunity to

Booker T. Washington, a former slave, founded Tuskegee Institute in 1881. He believed that African Americans would benefit most from vocational education.

earn a dollar in a factory just now is worth . . . more than the opportunity to spend a dollar in an opera house."[7]

Hundreds of young African Americans came to Tuskegee because it offered a realistic and reasonably quick way to make an economic place for themselves in the world. Though the school thrived under Washington's leadership, some blacks thought he gave up too much in order to win white support. Emerging leaders like W.E.B. Du Bois argued that Tuskegee trained African Americans for a permanently subordinate role in society.

W.E.B. Du Bois and the Quest for Equality

W.E.B. Du Bois was born on February 23, 1868, in the small town of Great Barrington, Massachusetts. Because he was born after the Civil War, he never experienced slavery, nor did he lack for education. He went to good schools where he distinguished himself as a brilliant student.

Ability alone was not enough to protect him from racial discrimination. As the only African-American child in what he called "a wee wooden schoolhouse" in Great Barrington, Du Bois soon learned about that discrimination:

> Something put it into the boys' and girls' heads to buy gorgeous visiting-cards—ten cents a package—and exchange [them]. The exchange was merry, till one girl, a tall newcomer, refused my card. . . . Then it dawned upon me with a certain suddenness that I was different from the others . . . shut out from their world by a vast veil."[8]

That veil did not stop Du Bois from going ahead with his education. He went on to graduate from Fisk University, an African-American school. In 1895, he became the first African American in history to earn a Ph.D. from Harvard University.

Du Bois became a professor at Atlanta University, meaning to settle into the quiet life of a scholar. Instead, he was drawn into the struggle for African-American rights. W.E.B. Du Bois admired the accomplishments of Booker T. Washington. But he was outraged that Washington told African Americans to make their peace with Jim Crow laws, stop pressing for voting rights, and accept their role as laborers and servants in a white-controlled society. According to Du Bois:

> Mr. Washington represents in Negro thought the old attitude of adjustment and submission. . . . [his] program practically accepts the alleged inferiority of the Negro races.[9]

Du Bois would not support such a program. In 1905, he gathered a group of African-American leaders and white supporters in Niagara Falls, Canada, to form what came to be known as the Niagara Movement.

With another black activist, William Monroe Trotter, Du Bois wrote a "Declaration of Principles" for the new organization. It was a ringing call for equality and human dignity. It was also a promise that African Americans would not give up the struggle until they had achieved justice:

We refuse to allow the impression to remain that the Negro American assents to inferiority, is submissive under oppression, and apologetic before insults. Through helplessness we may submit, but the voice of protest of 10 million Americans must never cease to assail the ears of their fellows so long as America is unjust.[10]

The Niagara Movement did not last long. Whites feared its militant activism. Booker T. Washington saw it as a threat to his policy of trading civil rights for economic opportunity. The organization itself was beset by quarrels and rivalries. By 1909, even Du Bois had to admit that the Niagara Movement was a lost cause.

The end of the Niagara Movement did not mean the end of civil rights activism. A new organization, the National Association for the Advancement of Colored People (NAACP), carried many of its principles forward.

2

Beginnings of the Movement

In the early twentieth century, with slavery two generations in the past, the white majority still expected African Americans to settle for less. A generation of new leaders refused to do that. Men like W.E.B. Du Bois, Marcus Garvey, and A. Philip Randolph told the people that true freedom was more the absence of slavery. It was equality before the law and recognition of the right of African Americans to control their own lives.

NAACP: The Way of Racial Integration

The NAACP began at a time of mounting racial violence, with lynchings and race riots turning once-peaceful communities into combat zones. Lynchings occurred mainly in the rural South, while race riots were more common in the cities of the North. Both involved mob violence.

Lynching is the public murder of individuals by mobs seeking revenge for some real or imagined misdeed. In the South, African Americans were lynched for petty offenses or simply for failing to be properly subservient to a white person. These people were killed in many ways—usually by hanging or shooting, but sometimes by burning or slow torture.

Riots are violent confrontations between groups. Most race riots began with white mobs attacking black neighborhoods. In August 1908, a three-day riot in Springfield, Illinois, played a major role in the formation of the NAACP.

The riot began when a black man was accused of attacking a white woman. When the sheriff transferred the man to a nearby town for safety, a white mob attacked the city's black neighborhood. Before the National Guard came to stop the fighting, six people were dead: two blacks and four whites. Many African Americans had been dragged out of their homes and severely beaten.

The outbreak of violence in the hometown of Abraham Lincoln convinced many people that something had to be done. On February 12, 1909—the hundredth anniversary of Abraham Lincoln's birth—a group of black activists and white supporters gathered to form a civil rights organization that would not be limited by gender or race. Men and women, black and white, would be welcome. In addition to A. Philip

Randolph, the NAACP founders included people such as antilynching crusader Ida Wells-Barnett, philosopher John Dewey, social worker Jane Addams, and W.E.B. Du Bois.

From the beginning of its organizational life, the NAACP did not limit itself to speeches, rallies, and moral arguments against racism. It planned to challenge Jim Crow laws in the courts. The leaders knew this would take time. Chipping away at one unjust law after another would not provide overnight solutions to the problems of African Americans.

The NAACP set to work. One of its earliest cases challenged "grandfather clauses." These laws

Lynching—illegal execution by a mob—was more common in the rural South than in the North. Black people were lynched for real or imagined offenses, often in front of hundreds of onlookers.

attempted to get around Fifteenth Amendment guarantees of voting rights to all citizens, regardless of race.

They took advantage of the fact that the amendment did not forbid all voter eligibility requirements, only those based on race. For example, states could require voters to demonstrate the ability to read.

Grandfather clauses waived these tests for those whose fathers or grandfathers had been eligible to vote before the Fifteenth Amendment took effect. Of course, African Americans could not qualify for the exemption. Thus, illiterate whites could vote while illiterate blacks could not.

The NAACP challenged these discriminatory laws in the case of *Guinn* v. *United States*. On June 21, 1915, the U.S. Supreme Court found the grandfather clauses unconstitutional.

With the *Guinn* ruling, the NAACP scored a significant victory. Not only did the case correct an injustice, it also showed that legal action could advance the cause of civil rights.

The Great Migration and the Harlem Renaissance

Though legal action worked, it did not work quickly. During the second decade of the twentieth century, thousands of African Americans simply did not have time to wait for the South to change. Many African Americans lived in grinding poverty, made worse by Jim Crow laws that denied them opportunities open to even the poorest whites. In the second decade of the twentieth century, the agricultural economy of the South floundered. The dreaded boll weevil attacked the cotton fields, destroying much of the crop. Cotton revenues dropped. Meanwhile, the industrialized North prospered as never before. In 1914, World War I began in Europe. This created a whole new industry in the American North, as factories geared up to supply war materiel to Great Britain and its allies.

All that production created a labor shortage, which grew even more critical when the United States entered the war in 1917. African Americans who earned as little as fifty cents a day in the cotton fields of the South could move north and earn as much as five dollars per day.

Between 1915 and 1930, about 2 million southern blacks headed north. This Great Migration, as it came to be called, redistributed the African-American population of America. For example, between 1910 and 1930, New York City's African-American population grew from 100,000 to 330,000, an increase of more than 300 percent.[1]

"We'd heard all about how the North was freer," remembered jazz musician Sidney Bechet, "and we were wanting to go real bad."[2] This great movement of people produced what came to be known as the Harlem Renaissance, or rebirth.

Harlem was the New York City neighborhood that became a center of African-American culture in the 1920s. It produced writers, poets, actors, musicians, and artists. It also produced scholars and social reformers.

These were the people that W.E.B. Du Bois called

"the Talented Tenth"—the top 10 percent of the African-American population. He believed that they could create a better life for blacks and all people of color.

Du Bois and many other top leaders believed that integration and equality would bring this better life. African Americans would take their place as equals in the white world. Others had a different vision. Instead of trying to fit in to a white society that would never welcome them, they wanted to build a new black nation.

Marcus Garvey: The Way of Black Nationalism

Marcus Garvey became one of the earliest proponents of black nationalism. He dreamed of leading American blacks to Africa, to create a country of their own. Their culture would flower. Their leaders would rule. Racism would become a thing of the past.

The Jamaican-born Garvey was a colorful figure with a taste for elaborate uniforms and a talent for appealing to a crowd. He moved to Harlem in 1917, with a big dream and a small organization: the Universal Negro Improvement Association (UNIA). With his inspiring street-corner oratory, he soon won an enthusiastic following. He built an ambitious program for black advancement on three principles: economic self-reliance, political self-determination, and the founding of a black nation in Africa. "There shall be no solution to this race problem until you

During the Harlem Renaissance, art and culture among African Americans flourished. Zora Neale Hurston was a well-known author and folklorist who influenced many later writers.

yourselves strike the blow for liberty," he once told his followers.[3]

UNIA's best-known project was the Black Star Line—a shipping company to be owned by black stockholders and staffed by black employees. On September 17, 1919, Black Star bought its first cargo ship, the SS *Yarmouth*, which it planned to rename SS *Frederick Douglass* in honor of the great abolitionist.

The ship and others that followed it would compete with other maritime shipping companies, transporting cargo across the Atlantic. When the time was right, these same ships would transport thousands of black Americans to Africa, where they would build their new nation.

The whole African-American community took pride in the Black Star Line. It brought many new members into the UNIA, making it the largest black nationalist organization in the country. When Marcus Garvey announced the first International Convention of the Negro Peoples of the World, people flocked to New York to attend.

The convention adopted a flag for the nation it planned to create in Africa, elected Marcus Garvey "provisional president" of that nation, and wrote a statement of UNIA principles.

It contained a list of grievances followed by a Declaration of Rights. It said that "all men, women and children of our blood throughout the world . . . [are] free citizens of Africa, the Motherland of all Negroes."[4]

The dream of a new black nation in Africa never

came to reality, nor did Black Star become a profitable shipping line. The company went out of business in April 1922. Less than a year later, on January 31, 1923, the UNIA office closed because the organization could no longer pay the rent.

Marcus Garvey himself ran into legal troubles and also managed to anger leaders like W.E.B. Du Bois. In May 1924, Du Bois's editorial in the NAACP magazine *The Crisis* called Garvey a "lunatic or traitor."[5]

In 1923, the government charged him with mail fraud because of his methods of selling stock in Black Star. After he had served three years of a five-year sentence, the government deported him to Jamaica. He died there on June 10, 1940.

In spite of his troubles, Marcus Garvey remained a hero to many African Americans. Though the UNIA disbanded and the Black Star Line failed, Garvey's work would have an important influence on the future. His call for black consciousness and pride helped to inspire the civil rights movement. The idea of black nationalism also survived, to be picked up later by an organization called the Nation of Islam.

Black Nationalism and the Nation of Islam

Founded in 1930 by Wallace Fard, the Nation of Islam adopted the Muslim religion and a program of economic self-help. Black Muslims, as outsiders often called them, wanted to be independent of whites. They began by rejecting Christianity, calling it a "white man's religion." Instead, they adopted the Islamic faith, which flourished in the African homeland.

Social and economic programs included creating black businesses and buying large parcels of land in the Deep South. On this land, they built their own communities and set up paramilitary forces to protect them.

In 1934, Wallace Fard disappeared under mysterious circumstances. Neither the authorities nor his followers ever found out what happened to him. His second in command, Elijah Muhammad, took over leadership of the movement.

Like Fard before him, Elijah Muhammad called for blacks to establish a separate nation, build a strong identity as a people, and become economically independent of white society. Muhammad led the Nation of Islam through the civil rights turmoil of the fifties and sixties. He died in 1975.

A. Philip Randolph and the Rights of Labor

Born in Crescent City, Florida, on April 15, 1889, Asa Philip Randolph was the son of an African Methodist Episcopal (AME) minister. As a "preacher's kid," Asa not only learned the Bible, he also learned about social activism. His father taught him that African Americans should struggle for their political and social rights. When he grew up, Asa Randolph decided to focus on the labor movement. Good jobs and decent pay seemed to him like a good place to start that struggle.

He also believed that labor unions could bring black and white workers together in a common cause: "The labor movement has been the home of the working man, and . . . [a] haven for the dispossessed. . . . I have tried to build an alliance between the Negro and the American labor movement."[6]

In 1925, Randolph helped to organize the nation's first all-black labor union: the Brotherhood of Sleeping Car Porters (BSCP). Sleeping cars were like rolling hotel suites, with private compartments and personal service around the clock. African-American porters in crisp white jackets provided that service. They worked for the Pullman Company, which owned and operated the cars.

When a group of porters decided to seek higher wages and better working conditions, they turned to A. Philip Randolph. At an organizational meeting on August 25, 1925, the BSCP was born. Asa Philip Randolph became its president.

The Pullman Company refused to recognize the new union. It fired some people and intimidated others. A. Philip Randolph and the BSCP held firm.

They tried without success to get the Interstate Commerce Commission to pressure the company for better wages. Later, Congress passed laws to protect railroad workers, but a loophole prevented those laws from applying to the Pullman porters.

Finally, in 1934, Congress closed the loophole. The BSCP won the right to appeal to the National Mediation Board. After hearing the case, the board ordered the company to allow the porters to vote on whether or not they wanted the BSCP to represent them. The union received 5,931 votes out of an

Sleeping-car porters provided service on trains. In 1925, they organized a union, led by A. Philip Randolph.

eligible 8,316.[7] The Pullman Company had to deal with the BSCP.

On August 25, 1937, the Brotherhood of Sleeping Car Porters became the first African-American union to sign a labor contract with a major American company. A. Philip Randolph and his people chose the date carefully. It was the twelfth anniversary of their first meeting in 1925.

The historic contract won Randolph a national reputation. He used it to win other victories for African-American workers. For example, in 1941 he convinced President Franklin D. Roosevelt to ban racial discrimination in hiring for government and defense industry jobs.

Integrating the Military

In 1948, Randolph achieved another major goal on the road to equality: He helped to persuade President Harry S. Truman to desegregate the United States military. During World War II and earlier, African-American soldiers had served in segregated units, commanded by white officers.

African-American soldiers often found themselves assigned to menial labor. They also suffered because many whites, especially in the South, feared nothing so much as a black man with a gun.

This racism could become vicious for the slightest reason, or sometimes for no reason at all. For example, angry whites in Mississippi brutalized African-American soldiers returning from World War II. An outraged President Truman strongly condemned this behavior:

> My very stomach turned over when I learned that Negro soldiers, just back from overseas, were being dumped out of army trucks . . . and beaten. Whatever my [feelings about race] might have been, as President I know this is bad. I shall fight to end evils like this.[8]

Truman kept his word. On July 26, 1948, he issued an executive order banning racial discrimination in the military.

Advances like this helped the African-American cause, but they did not solve the root problems of inequality. Racism still limited black opportunities. Jim Crow segregation still flourished in the South. Ending it would be the long and dangerous task of the civil rights movement that began in the 1950s.

3

Challenging Jim Crow Segregation

The second half of the twentieth century began on a high note for civil rights activists. A 1950 Supreme Court ruling opened new doors for the NAACP in its struggle against segregated education.

The case began in 1946, when African-American student Herman Sweatt sued the University of Texas Law School, which had refused to admit him on racial grounds. Thurgood Marshall of the NAACP Legal Defense Fund handled the case.

Targeting *Plessy* v. *Ferguson*

The *Plessy* v. *Ferguson* decision of 1896 established the idea of "separate but equal" facilities for the races. It became the foundation for Jim Crow laws all over the South. The NAACP had been fighting it for years.

Marshall, an African-American lawyer, found a way to use *Plessy* to his client's advantage. He pointed out that facilities for blacks had to be equal to those for whites. Texas had no law schools for African Americans. Therefore, Fourteenth Amendment guarantees of equal protection under the law should require the university to admit Herman Sweatt and other black students.

The argument frightened Texas segregationists. It was a good one and they knew it. They tried to block it with a hastily created law school for blacks. The plan fell through because the new school would not have been equal to the university law school.

In the Supreme Court opinion, Chief Justice Frank Vinson pointed out:

> The University of Texas Law School . . . was staffed by a faculty of sixteen full-time and three part-time professors. . . . Its student body numbered 850. The library contained over 65,000 volumes. . . .
>
> The law school for Negroes which was to have opened in February, 1947, would have had no independent faculty or library. The teaching was to be carried on by four members of the University of Texas Law School faculty, who [would be] teaching at both institutions.[1]

The white Texans tried again. They failed when another proposal did not meet the equality test. On

Under the Jim Crow laws, whites and blacks were separated in many daily activities. Facilities for African Americans—from fountains to colleges—were usually inferior to those for whites.

June 5, 1950, the Court ordered that Sweatt be admitted to the University of Texas Law School.

Sweatt v. *Painter* did not attack all segregated education. It succeeded by working within the restrictions of *Plessy* v. *Ferguson*.

The next step would be a challenge to the whole idea of "separate but equal" education. The NAACP meant to prove that racial segregation itself made schools unequal—and therefore unconstitutional. This meant going head-to-head against *Plessy* v. *Ferguson*.

Mounting the Challenge

Shortly after the *Sweatt* victory, the NAACP received requests for legal help from plaintiffs in Kansas, South Carolina, Virginia, and Delaware. All the cases involved blacks attending segregated public schools. When the cases came before the Supreme Court in

1952, they were grouped together under the title *Brown* v. *Board of Education of Topeka, Kansas.*

The NAACP legal team chose *Brown* as the lead case after much careful thought. In South Carolina, Virginia, and Delaware, African-American schools were clearly inferior. In Kansas, they were nearly equal to white schools. They had similar facilities, teacher training, class size, and spending per pupil.

This would allow the NAACP to focus on segregation itself. Lead counsel Thurgood Marshall knew that a hard task lay ahead. He and his team carefully worked out their strategy.

They based the argument on Fourteenth Amendment guarantees of equal rights for all citizens, African Americans included. Segregated schooling was unequal by its very nature. Therefore, schools should be integrated.

To prove the point, they introduced a psychological study. Social psychologist Kenneth B. Clark worked with two hundred African-American children of various ages. His method was simple and revealing. Clark placed white and black dolls before each child and asked him or her to choose the prettiest doll, the ugliest doll, the doll the child liked best. Children as young as three years old preferred the white dolls. They called the black dolls ugly.

From the study, Clark concluded that segregation did indeed damage African-American children. Segregated schooling marked them as inferior to whites and therefore could never give them a truly equal education.

When *Brown* v. *Board of Education* was first

argued in December 1952, the justices could not reach agreement. Some did not want to hand down a verdict that would probably have to be enforced by armed troops. They also disliked the idea of overturning *Plessy* v. *Ferguson*. Supreme Court justices do not lightly set aside the rulings of previous courts.

Chief Justice Fred Vinson could not pull the court together. Justice Felix Frankfurter suggested calling for a reargument to clarify certain points of law. The other justices readily agreed.

A year later, in December 1953, Thurgood Marshall and the NAACP legal team again appeared before the Supreme Court. This time, Marshall faced a new chief justice. Fred Vinson had died, and in his place was Earl Warren, former governor of California.

Warren was a politician rather than a legal scholar. He knew how to find agreement among people with opposing viewpoints. He also knew what the law could and could not do. Often he had heard it argued that the law could not wipe out racial prejudice because it could not change people's beliefs. To this argument, he made a straightforward reply: "True, prejudice cannot be wiped out, but infliction of it upon others can."[2]

The reargument convinced Warren that the time had come to correct the injustices of the past. He knew that overturning *Plessy* would trigger a massive struggle that would be long, painful, and quite probably violent. If the Court handed down a divided opinion, it would only make the situation worse.

Earl Warren wanted an overwhelming majority. He contacted his fellow justices one by one and spoke

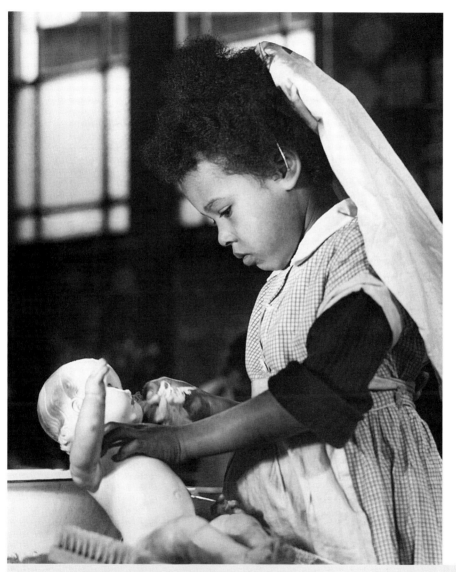

Psychologist Kenneth Clark found that African-American children preferred white dolls, saying that the black dolls were ugly. This led to the conclusion that segregation harmed children's self-esteem.

with them about their concerns. On May 17, 1954, he presented the majority opinion in the courtroom. There was no minority opinion: The decision of the Court in the matter of *Brown* v. *Board of Education of Topeka* was unanimous.

The chief justice surely knew that the people in the gallery were hanging on to his every word. He read slowly, deliberately, explaining the issues that the Court had considered. At last he reached the ruling. With scarcely a pause, he began to read:

> We come then to the question presented: Does segregation of children in public schools solely on the basis of race, even though the physical facilities and other "tangible" factors may be equal, deprive the children of the minority group of equal educational opportunities? *We believe that it does.*"[3] [emphasis added]

With those words, the Court overthrew *Plessy* v. *Ferguson*. The justices knew that this ruling was not an ending, but a beginning. Next came the hard part: putting it into effect.

The justices knew that desegregation would not happen quickly. They decided not to force the issue by setting a time limit. The ruling simply said that integration should be accomplished "with all deliberate speed." The vague wording allowed some school districts to stall, but it still affirmed that school integration must take place.

By discarding *Plessy*, the Court had not only transformed public education. It had also knocked the supports out from under the whole Jim Crow system. *Brown* would begin in the schools, but it would not stop there: The days of sitting in the back of the bus and drinking at "colored" fountains were numbered.

A Grim Legacy

While the Court worked out rules for desegregation, white rage in the South made the lives of black people even more difficult. Under the wrong conditions, things could turn deadly very quickly.

In August 1955, the fate of fourteen-year-old Emmett Till stunned the entire country. The Chicago-born Till was a bright, energetic boy with an engaging grin and a streak of mischief. He had known prejudice and discrimination in Chicago, but never the rigid racial etiquette of the South.

Before Till and his cousin Curtis Jones went to visit relatives in Mississippi, his mother warned him to be on his guard and "behave himself." No one knows how seriously he took her warnings; like most boys his age, he probably did not pay much attention.

The boys stayed with their great-uncle, Moses Wright, an elderly sharecropper in Tallahatchie County. Exactly what happened has never been clear. Apparently, Till and Jones were playing with some local boys in front of a grocery store. Till began bragging that he had dated white girls in Chicago.

The local boys scoffed; never could they believe such a thing. They dared Till to prove his skill with white females by going into the store and flirting with twenty-one-year-old Carolyn Bryant. Bryant and her husband, Roy, owned the store. Most of their customers were African-American sharecroppers.

Emmett Till, a fourteen-year-old from Chicago, was a victim of white rage in Mississippi. His tragedy stunned the nation.

Till took the dare. He went into the store to buy candy. By some accounts, he whistled at Carolyn Bryant. By others, he said "Bye, baby" as he left the store. Bryant later claimed that he touched her.

Roy Bryant and his half brother J. W. Milam hunted down Emmett Till and beat him, crushing his head. Then they shot him and threw his body into the Tallahatchie River. Searchers found it three days later. The body was so badly disfigured that Moses Wright had to identify it from a ring Till wore.

Till's body was shipped home for burial. His mother demanded an open casket funeral, so the world would see "what they did to my boy."[4]

The world saw, and the world was horrified. Thousands filed into the African-American funeral home to view the body. Coming as it did only fifteen months after *Brown*, the brutal murder became a symbol of violent racism in the segregated South.

Reporters from major papers all over the country covered the trial of Bryant and Milam. To the disgust and dismay of the media, the government, and ordinary citizens all over the country, a white jury took just over one hour to find the defendants not guilty of killing Emmett Till.

The Till case turned a media spotlight on the South just as it was entering what came to be called the "civil rights era." That spotlight would not go away. The nation would watch on TV as African Americans fought for the rights that had so long been denied them.

4

Montgomery, Alabama: The Bus Boycott

The story has been told so often, it has become a legend—how Rosa Parks, an African-American seamstress in Montgomery, Alabama, refused to give up her seat to a white man on a city bus. By law, African-American passengers had to sit in the back of the bus. Montgomery buses did not have a clearly defined line between sections. If the bus became crowded, the driver could change the dividing line by ordering black passengers to give up their seats to whites.

This is what happened to Rosa Parks on December 1, 1955. The driver, J. F. Blake, ordered her to give her seat to a white man who had just boarded the bus. It happened all the time in Montgomery. But this time, things were different.

Drawing the Line in Montgomery

Rosa Parks said no. The driver bullied and badgered her, then threatened to have her arrested. Still, she said no. True to his word, J. F. Blake called the police. They arrested Rosa Parks for breaking the segregation laws.

The forty-two-year-old Parks was a respected member of Montgomery's African-American community and secretary of the local NAACP chapter. J. F. Blake and the Montgomery police had just handed the group a perfect test case.

Civil rights activists had wanted to challenge Montgomery's bus segregation laws ever since *Brown* v. *Board of Education* knocked out the legal foundation of Jim Crow. Local black leader E. D. Nixon and white activist Clifford Durr asked Rosa Parks if she would be that test case.

Parks well knew the dangers of defying the white establishment. Still, she said yes.

From Lawsuit to Boycott

Everybody knew a lawsuit would take time, a long time, with trials and verdicts and appeals that might go all the way to the Supreme Court. The public outrage over Rosa Parks's arrest would be gone by then. The time was ripe for immediate action.

The idea of a bus boycott seems to have occurred

to several different people at almost the same time. College professor Jo Ann Hall got together with some other faculty members at Alabama State College. They wrote a letter of protest to distribute through the whole community:

> Another Negro woman has been arrested and thrown into jail because she refused to get up out of her seat on the bus and give it to a white person. . . . Until we do something to stop these arrests, they will continue. . . . This woman's case will come up Monday. We are, therefore, asking every Negro to stay off the buses on Monday in protest of the arrest and trial.[1]

E. D. Nixon called a meeting of community leaders to discuss the options. The new minister of the Dexter Avenue Baptist Church, Martin Luther King, Jr., said the group could meet in the church basement.

They gathered on Friday evening. King and a few others wrote a leaflet to circulate through the community. It asked every African American in Montgomery to avoid riding buses on Monday: "take a cab, or share a ride, or walk," it said.[2]

The boycott planners spent a tense, sleepless weekend. They had no idea what to expect on Monday morning. Martin Luther King, Jr., and his wife, Coretta, were up before daylight, eager to see what would happen.

Coretta King stood by the window, peering out into the predawn grayness. At last she saw the approaching lights of a Montgomery city bus. As it moved past the house, she could see inside. It was empty! Normally, that bus was almost full by the time it passed the house.

King jumped in his car and began driving around town. Everywhere he looked the buses were empty or occupied by a handful of white riders. The boycott was succeeding far beyond anything the organizers had foreseen.

Many people, including King, wanted to extend the boycott and use it to demand complete desegregation of Montgomery's buses. The African-American community was united and ready. So long as they remained united, they could play havoc with the bus system, simply by staying away. About 75 percent of bus customers were African-American. The system could not stay in business for long without them.

The leaders decided to form a new organization to manage the boycott. They called it the Montgomery Improvement Association (MIA), and elected Martin Luther King, Jr., as its president. That night, King addressed the rally, setting the tone for what lay ahead:

> I want to say that we are not here advocating violence. We have never done that. . . . The only weapon that we have in our hands this evening is the weapon of protest. That's all. . . . My friends, I want it to be known that we're going to work with grim and bold determination to gain justice on the buses in this city.
>
> And we are not wrong; we are not wrong in what we are doing. If we are wrong, the Supreme Court of this nation is wrong. If we are wrong, the Constitution of the United States is wrong. If we are wrong, God Almighty is wrong. . . . If we are wrong, justice is a lie. . . . And we are determined

here in Montgomery to work and fight until justice runs down like water, and righteousness like a mighty stream.[3]

Preparing for the Difficulties Ahead

While King and the Montgomery Improvement Association focused on the boycott, attorney Fred Gray got busy on appeals for Rosa Parks. Both actions would stretch over more than a year.

It was not an easy thing the people had chosen to

When Rosa Parks was arrested and jailed for refusing to give up her seat to a white man, it prompted a boycott of Birmingham buses by the African-American community. Here Parks is being fingerprinted after her arrest.

do. The bus system was their economic lifeline. Most had no other way to get to work.

In the first few days of the boycott, African-American taxi drivers did their part. They filled their cabs with passengers who paid only ten cents each—the cost of a bus ride. That ended when the white police commissioner threatened to arrest any taxi driver who cut his fares.

King went to work organizing a massive, city-wide carpool. At a rally, he asked people with cars to volunteer as drivers. About 150 came forward.

Even with that help, there were not enough cars to go around. Some people had to walk long distances while empty city buses rolled past them in the streets. What began in a rush of enthusiasm grew into a test of endurance.

To keep up morale, the MIA held mass meetings. People gathered to sing, to pray, to vent their frustrations and celebrate their victories. And there were victories: small acts of personal courage that deserved notice.

African-American churches hosted these meetings. In the black community, churches were not only centers of spiritual life, but of social life as well. Whole families participated in everything from Sunday worship services to midweek choir practices and Friday night suppers.

Ministers held a special position of honor within the community. It was no accident that many of the early civil rights leaders were clergymen: Martin Luther King, Jr., Ralph Abernathy, and Fred Shuttlesworth, to name a few. Their participation in the boycott and other civil rights activities gave the people courage.

The Long Haul

Even with community commitment, the daily grind of the boycott was punishing. Some people left home before dawn so they could walk to work by 8:00 A.M. Some paid more for groceries because they had to buy more expensive small sizes so they could carry their purchases home.

One elderly woman, known to all as "Mother Pollard," would hobble to the store and back again, lugging her packages. Several people tried to get her to drop out of the boycott because of her advanced age. Mother Pollard was having none of that: "My feets is weary, but my soul is rested," she said.[4]

That one sentence would be repeated over and over again in the weeks and months to come. It inspired countless boycotters to continue on the hard road they had chosen.

The road was not only difficult, but also tricky and sometimes dangerous. Talks with white leaders led nowhere. They agreed that drivers should be more courteous to black passengers. They even agreed that the shifting dividing line between sections was a problem. But they would not even discuss desegregating the buses.

While King and the MIA negotiating team were bogged down in politics, attorney Fred Gray had problems of his own. Rosa Parks's appeal was stalled in the state courts.

Gray wanted to file a class action suit in federal court. The suit would not deal with discourteous drivers and shifting dividing lines. It would challenge the entire policy of segregation on Montgomery's city buses. With the separate-but-equal doctrine of *Plessy* overturned, the time seemed ripe.

The MIA agreed and Fred Gray set to work. For him, the case that would come to be known as *Browder* v. *Gayle* was the dream of a lifetime. An Alabama native, Gray left his home state to go to college. There he made a secret vow that would shape the rest of his life: "to become a lawyer, return to Alabama, and destroy everything segregated I could find."[5]

Browder v. *Gayle* gave him a chance to do that. He chose Aurelia Browder as his lead plaintiff. Like Rosa Parks, Browder was a seamstress who had been arrested for refusing to surrender her seat on a city bus.

While the case worked its way through the courts, the boycott heated up. Frustrated whites struck out at what they saw as a threat to their way of life.

On January 30, 1956, someone firebombed King's house while he was at a meeting. Fortunately, his wife and daughter were not hurt in the blast. An angry crowd gathered in the street, calling for revenge on the white people of Montgomery.

No, said Martin Luther King, Jr. To keep the moral high ground, they must not strike out in anger.

Officials in Montgomery did not throw bombs. They used more "civilized" means to cripple the boycott. Police harassed African-American motorists with citations for minor offenses. City officials sued in state court to get the carpool banned. They claimed it was an unlicensed city transportation system.

On November 13, 1956, Martin Luther King, Jr., and other MIA leaders were in court, listening to arguments on the carpool case. Everyone knew the judge would rule against the MIA.

Then, news came from Washington, D.C.: the Supreme Court had ruled in *Browder* v. *Gayle*, striking down bus segregation laws as unconstitutional. The courtroom erupted.

The judge restored order just long enough to issue an injunction against the carpool. It had to disband immediately. Even many whites who supported segregation recognized that as a spiteful act.

Integration did not begin until the Supreme Court order had been served on Montgomery officials. Finally, on December 20, Martin Luther King, Jr., led a group of blacks and whites onto a Montgomery city bus. They sat together in front, as if that was the way things had always been.

White Anger

That moment of joyous triumph was not the end of the story in Montgomery. Several times, snipers fired shotguns at integrated buses. In the predawn hours of January 10, bombs exploded at two homes and four churches. Two weeks later, a bomb went off near King's home, destroying a taxi stand. Three drivers were injured by shattering glass. Another bomb was placed on King's porch. Only a sputtering fuse kept it from exploding.

Fred Shuttlesworth, Ralph Abernathy, and Martin Luther King, Jr. (shown left to right) were three clergymen who used nonviolence to attack segregation and discrimination.

Montgomery would survive this period of violence. However, it became clear that new laws were only a first step. Next, African Americans and their supporters faced the larger, and far more dangerous, challenge of putting those laws into practice.

Southern politicians made it clear that they had no intention of making that process easy. On March 12, 1956, 101 members of congress from the eleven states of the old confederacy signed a manifesto, or declaration of principles. It called for resistance to all racial integration.

Under the title "Declaration of Constitutional Principles," the manifesto appealed to *Plessy* v. *Ferguson*, noting that

> the Supreme Court . . . declared that under the Fourteenth Amendment no person was denied any of his rights if the states provided separate-but-equal public facilities. . . . This interpretation, restated time and again, became a part of the life of the people of many of the states and confirmed their habits, customs, traditions, and way of life.

The manifesto went on to praise "those states which have declared the intention to resist forced integration by any lawful means."[6] However, the violent reaction in Montgomery was one of many indications that opponents of segregation would not limit themselves to lawful dissent.

The Southern Christian Leadership Conference

In 1957, Martin Luther King, Jr., and other veterans of the Montgomery boycott founded the Southern Christian Leadership Conference (SCLC). The organization advocated what it called "Christian nonviolence" and worked closely with African-American churches.

According to King, SCLC worked through churches "because of the very structure of the Negro community in the South."[7] The connection to the church and the commitment to nonviolent social action put SCLC's work into moral terms.

At the founding conference on January 11, 1957, the group wrote its own manifesto. It called the treatment of African Americans in the South "a basic spiritual problem" and vowed that in the struggle, "not one hair of one head of one white person shall be harmed."[8]

With competing manifestos, the line was drawn between black and white. The two sides could not have been further apart. For all the differences, the white congressmen who signed the "Declaration of Constitutional Principles" and the black clergymen who signed the SCLC Manifesto did have one thing in common: Both believed wholeheartedly in what they were doing.

5

Pioneers in School Integration

Integrating schools was even more difficult than integrating buses. Many white parents taught their children that whites were naturally superior to blacks. Mixing the races at school would send a message of equality. All over the South, communities vowed to fight school desegregation to the bitter end.

African Americans realized that making a law was one thing; having that law enforced and put into practice was quite another. If school integration was going to happen at all, African Americans had to take an active role in making it happen. They knew that the struggle would take courage.

Integrating the University of Alabama

Personal courage was not always rewarded with victory in that struggle. For example, in 1956 a young woman named Autherine Lucy applied to the University of Alabama school of library science. Though she was well qualified for the program, the university turned her down.

Lucy went to the NAACP for help. The legal department considered her case fairly routine. They had been integrating graduate schools since *Sweatt* in 1950, without violence or mob protests.

When they got a court injunction forcing the university to admit Autherine Lucy, they felt confident that she would be allowed to begin classes without difficulty. This time, they were wrong.

On February 3, 1956, Lucy formally enrolled at the university. On her third day of classes, she walked onto the campus and into a nightmare. Mobs of screaming whites pelted her with eggs and blocked her way into the building. It took a police escort to get her to classes that day.

The university took no action against the mob. Instead it suspended and later expelled Autherine Lucy. Many years later, Lucy would reflect on her experience: "They were fighting tradition and change. It just wasn't my time," she said.[1] It would be another seven years before the University of Alabama was successfully integrated.

The Little Rock Nine

The Alabama cases involved adults seeking admission to a university. In September 1957, the first great crisis in public school integration burst upon Little Rock, Arkansas. For many who were involved in desegregation, the sheer fury of public reaction came as a surprise. Arkansas had a national reputation as a racially moderate state.

Little Rock's buses and public libraries had already been integrated, with only token protests. School superintendent Virgil T. Blossom planned for gradual integration, beginning with one high school in 1957 and working down to first grade by 1963. The school board supported the plan and decided to start with Central High School.

The board chose seventeen African-American students to enter Central. By September, eight had dropped out of the program. Three boys and six girls remained. Their names were Ernest Green, Elizabeth Eckford, Jefferson Thomas, Terrence Roberts, Carlotta Walls, Minnijean Brown, Gloria Ray, Thelma Mothershed, and Melba Pattillo.

School started on September 4, 1957. Daisy Bates, president of the Arkansas NAACP, arranged for the nine to go as a group. She asked several black and white ministers to escort them. A police car stood by in case of trouble.

On the morning of the fourth, the students gathered at Bates's house. One girl was missing. Because her family did not have a telephone, fifteen-year-old Elizabeth Eckford had not gotten the message about going as a group. The eight students and their escorts set out for school.

A mob of angry whites waited for them, and Arkansas National Guardsmen surrounded the building. The students thought the Guard was there to protect them. They soon found out that Governor Orval E. Faubus had sent the Guard to keep them out of Central High.

With Guardsmen barring the way and the crowd screaming threats, the clergymen got the students out as quickly as they could. After they had gone, Elizabeth Eckford arrived alone. She later recalled:

> The crowd was quiet. I guess they were waiting to see what was going to happen. . . . When I was able to steady my knees, I walked up to the guard who had let the white students in. . . . he raised his bayonet and then the other guards moved in

Elizabeth Eckford, one of the Little Rock Nine, endured taunts and threats from white students and adults when she tried to attend Central High School.

and they raised their bayonets. They glared at me with a mean look and I was very frightened and I didn't know what to do. I turned around and the crowd came toward me."[2]

Eckford made her way to a bus bench in front of the school. She said, "A white man sat down beside me, put his arm around me and patted my shoulder. He raised my chin and said, 'Don't let them see you cry.'"[3] Two sympathetic white people helped her get on a bus and out of harm's way.

Federal Intervention

The NAACP went to court to get the Guardsmen removed. On September 20, Federal District Judge Ronald Davies ordered Governor Faubus to withdraw the Guard or face contempt of court charges.

With the Guardsmen gone, the nine again tried to enter Central High. On September 23, they slipped through a side door while police controlled the crowd.

When the crowd learned that the students were inside, it became so unruly that the police feared a full-scale riot. They smuggled out the African-American students and took them to their homes.

By this time, President Dwight D. Eisenhower decided he had had enough. On September 24, he ordered the troops of the 101st Airborne Division into Little Rock. He also placed the Arkansas National Guard under federal command.

That evening he addressed the nation to speak of "the sadness I feel in the action I was [forced] today to take and the firmness with which I intend to pursue this course until the orders of the federal court at Little Rock can be executed without unlawful interference."[4]

He also spoke of the damage to America's standing in the world:

> Our enemies are gloating over this incident and using it . . . to misrepresent our whole nation. We are portrayed as a violator of those standards of conduct . . . [proclaimed] in the Charter of the United Nations. There they affirmed "faith in fundamental human rights" and "in the dignity and worth of the human person" and they did so "without distinction as to race, sex, language or religion."[5]

Early the next morning, members of the 101st Airborne conducted the Little Rock Nine into Central High School. This time, the students were able to stay.

The Struggle Continues

Getting into the school was only the beginning. The next challenge was staying there. Every day brought new humiliations. White students taunted the nine and called them names. They attacked them, kicking, tripping, and hitting them from behind. A white student sprayed acid into Melba Pattillo's eyes.

On her sixteenth birthday, Pattillo wrote a telling entry in her diary: "Please, God, let me learn how to stop being a warrior. Sometimes I just need to be a girl."[6] She did not get that chance in the 1957–1958 school year.

None of the nine did, yet all but one made it through. Minnijean Brown could never quite control her anger. She had several run-ins with white students and was expelled in February 1958. There was also a success: On May 27, 1958, Ernest Green, the only senior in the original nine, became the first African American ever to graduate from Central High.

The Lost Year

To stop integration from continuing into the 1958–1959 school term, Governor Faubus issued a proclamation closing the schools in Little Rock. He then called a special election, asking voters to decide "for or against the proposition of racial integration of all schools within the school district."[7]

On September 27, 1958, 72 percent of those voters decided they would rather close the schools than open them to both races. Thus began what the students at Central High came to call the Lost Year.

Some parents sent their children to boarding schools or to relatives who lived outside the Little Rock School District. Others tried to open private schools. Options such as these were expensive and out of reach for many families. Hundreds of students, both black and white, had to struggle along as best they could.

Elizabeth Eckford took a correspondence course: "Since my parents were accustomed to paying for my books, this was not so difficult," she later told an interviewer.[8]

Little Rock's school desegregation crisis had unexpected repercussions. The whole state became something of a pariah, or outcast. To many people,

Children in elementary school also fought segregation. Ruby Bridges, a first-grader and the only black child at her school, had to be escorted to and from the building by federal marshals in New Orleans, Louisiana, in 1960.

Arkansas meant a teenage African-American girl, alone and unprotected in an angry mob. It meant combat troops at a high school and white parents who would rather destroy the schools than open them to blacks.

The economy suffered because the state could not attract new industry. There were suits and counter-suits, angry public forums, and shake-ups in the Little Rock School Board. White teenagers, confronted with the possibility of not getting their high school diplomas, demanded action.

Finally, on June 18, 1959, a U.S. District Court ruled Arkansas' school-closing law unconstitutional. The Little Rock School Board decided not to appeal the ruling. It announced that all schools would reopen in the fall, with the high schools integrated according to federal guidelines.

Reopening school did not solve Little Rock's racial problems. The Little Rock Nine had won a battle—a large and important battle, to be sure. But the war against school segregation in Arkansas had only just begun. It would be twelve long years before the Little Rock public schools achieved full integration.

6

The Beginnings of Sixties Activism

In the sixties, a different group of civil rights activists emerged. Most were college students who lacked the patience for long legal battles. They wanted to speed up the pace of change, and they were willing to take direct action to do it.

This new generation began finding its voice in 1960. It all started when four African-American college students walked into a Greensboro, North Carolina, dime store and sat down at the lunch counter.

The Greensboro Four

Franklin McCain, Joseph McNeil, David Richmond, and Ezell Blair, Jr., were still in

63

their teens when they launched what came to be known as the Greensboro sit-ins. The four young men lived in the same dormitory at North Carolina Agricultural and Technical University.

In many a late-night conversation, they shared their outrage over the Jim Crow laws that doomed them to second-class citizenship. At one of these gatherings, they decided that the time had come for action.

On February 1, 1960, they walked into the F. W. Woolworth's store in downtown Greensboro. They bought some school supplies and other small items, then sat down at the lunch counter. White customers stared in silent disbelief. The waitresses simply ignored them.

F. W. Woolworth's was a national chain that seg-regated its lunch counters only in the South. Rather than provide separate seating for African-American customers, the lunch counters did not serve them at all.

The four young demonstrators had expected anger, even violence. They had not expected silence. It puzzled them, but it did not discourage them. They kept trying to get someone to take their order.

Finally, one of the waitresses asked them to leave. The counter did not serve black people, she said. They were wasting their time. In the best traditions of nonviolent protest, the students were calm and courteous. They did not yell, spout obscenities, or threaten. But they also did not move.

The exasperated waitress called store manager Curly Harris to the scene. He also failed to convince these stubborn but unfailingly polite teenagers to leave. To get rid of them, he finally had to close the store.

The demonstrators left, promising Harris that they would be back the next morning. Many years later, he reflected on that first encounter with the Greensboro Four. His boss at Woolworth's headquarters told him not to worry. It would all blow over in a day or two. "I said, ain't about to blow over. . . . I said I don't think so. It's for real," Harris reported.[1]

Spreading the Word

Curly Harris was right: The sit-ins did not blow over, and the Greensboro Four did not go away. The news media got hold of the story and soon made the young protesters into celebrities.

When they came back, they were not alone. Sources differ about how many students showed up at Woolworth's to sit with the four. The number was probably somewhere around twenty, and each day saw more.

On Saturday, February 6, hundreds of African-American students descended on the downtown area. They were orderly, peaceful, and quietly determined. They had come to town for one reason: to serve notice on white Greensboro that things were about to change.

In the days and weeks to follow, cities all over the South got the same message. Within two months, sit-ins were taking place in fifty-four cities in nine states. What began with four teenagers who wanted to make a statement had turned into a grass roots civil rights movement of amazing power.

The Nashville Sit-ins

When Greensboro burst on the scene, black students in Nashville, Tennessee, had already started to prepare for sit-ins. A group of them studied nonviolent methods of social change with the Reverend Jim Lawson. Eight leaders emerged from those sessions— gifted young men and women who believed wholeheartedly in their cause.

Lawson himself had studied the work of Mohandas K. Gandhi, the legendary *mahatma*, or "great soul," of India. Gandhi's nonviolent strategies helped to win India's independence from Great Britain. When Greensboro made headlines, Lawson decided that the time was ripe for action.

On February 13, 1960, groups of neatly dressed black young people entered Woolworth's and two other stores in downtown Nashville. They made purchases and then sat down at the lunch counters. They tried to order, but the waitresses ignored them.

They sat for two hours, until the lunch counters closed. Then they got up quietly and left. This basic routine continued for ten days, while the downtown merchants grew more and more nervous. The sit-ins were attracting attention—and costing them business. Finally, on February 26, the police chief served notice: If the demonstrators returned, they would be arrested.

On Saturday, February 27—Big Saturday, as it

came to be called—the students marched into town and took up their positions at the various stores. The arrests soon began. By the end of the day, seventy-seven black and four white demonstrators had been loaded into a patrol wagon and taken off to jail.

On Monday, they were brought before the court. The judge began reading off a long list of guilty verdicts and fines. Before he could finish, student leader Diane Nash got to her feet and announced that some of the defendants had decided to go to jail rather than pay fines: "We feel that if we pay these fines we

Dorothy Bell, an African-American college student, waits to be served at a whites-only lunch counter in Birmingham, Alabama; she was later arrested. The sit-ins that began with four young men at the Woolworth's in Greensboro spread all over the South.

would be contributing to and supporting the injustice and immoral practices that have been performed in the arrest and conviction of the defendants."[2]

One by one, most of the other defendants followed Nash's example, announcing that they, too, would refuse to pay the fine. A stunned courtroom watched as Diane Nash and fifteen other defendants were led off to jail.

Thus the protesters turned even imprisonment into a tool of nonviolent resistance. They gave the judge no choice but to fill the jail with dozens of nonviolent, well-mannered college students whose only "crime" was trying to order a cup of coffee or a slice of pie.

SNCC: Taking the Moral High Ground

The "jail no bail" strategy became part of the arsenal for a new civil rights group: the Student Nonviolent Coordinating Committee, or SNCC (pronounced "snick"). SNCC was the first organization created by and for the younger generation of civil rights activists. It was also first to use the word "nonviolent" in its name as well as its statement of purpose.

In that statement, the founders of SNCC affirmed "the philosophical or religious ideal of nonviolence as the foundation of our purpose . . . our faith, and the manner of our action."[3] They also made it clear that *nonviolence* did not mean *nonaction*.

SNCC called for direct and vigorous action against segregation in all its forms. They wanted nothing less than to end Jim Crow and wipe out every trace of second-class citizenship for African Americans. The success of the sit-ins proved that nonviolent strategies could accomplish that task.

Communities all over the South yielded to the pressure. On May 10, 1960, Nashville became the first major city to begin desegregating public places. Woolworth's and several other retail chains formally desegregated all their stores, lunch counters included.

In Greensboro, North Carolina, July 25, 1960, was a memorable occasion. On that day, an African-American customer sat down at Woolworth's lunch counter and calmly ate a meal.

The Freedom Rides

A 1960 Supreme Court decision inspired the next major confrontation with Jim Crow. In 1946, the Court had banned discrimination in interstate travel. The ruling applied to buses, trains, and airplanes that traveled between states. The decision of December 5, 1960, extended the ban to interstate terminals. This meant that bus stations could no longer have separate facilities for the races. Everything from waiting rooms and diners to restrooms and water fountains had to be desegregated.

As usual, the ruling was one thing; putting it into practice was another. In the summer of 1961, the Congress of Racial Equality (CORE) set out to do that. It planned "Freedom Rides." Integrated teams of blacks and whites would travel through the South on regularly scheduled buses.

This was not a new thing for the Chicago-based

civil rights group. Founded in 1942 by James Farmer and other college students, CORE committed itself to nonviolent social action.

When the 1947 Supreme Court decision banned discrimination in interstate travel, CORE staged what it called a "Journey of Reconciliation." Eight black and eight white men would travel through the South, defying segregation laws on buses. Members of the team were arrested several times. A North Carolina judge sentenced two whites and two blacks to jail terms ranging from thirty to ninety days.

The Freedom Riders of 1960 expected more of the same, and worse. James Farmer organized the rides, planning to protest segregation in the most direct way possible. On the bus, blacks would sit in front and whites in back. In terminals, blacks would use the "white" facilities and vice versa. According to Farmer: "This was not civil disobedience really, because we [were] . . . doing what the Supreme Court said we had a right to do."[4]

The first two teams left Washington, D.C., on May 4, 1961. One traveled by Greyhound, the other by Continental Trailways. The protesters knew they had to be ready for anything: "I think all of us were prepared for as much violence as could be thrown at us. We were prepared for the possibility of death," Farmer recalled.[5]

The riders headed for New Orleans. They planned to arrive there on May 17, the seventh anniversary of the *Brown* decision. Neither group would make it through Alabama.

The little town of Anniston was a Ku Klux Klan

stronghold. The Klan, a violent racist organization, began after the Civil War. Dressed in white robes, with hoods to hide their features, Klansmen spread terror and death through African-American communities. Though eventually outlawed and disbanded, the Klan reappeared in the 1920s. It terrorized African Americans who showed signs of forgetting their "place." In the fifties and sixties, it targeted civil rights activists.

In Anniston, Klansmen waylaid the Greyhound bus. They slashed the tires and smashed windows with iron bars. Someone threw a bomb through the shattered back window. The passengers barely escaped with their lives as the bomb exploded and the bus burst into flames.

The riders lay sprawled on the ground, gasping for air. Help arrived before the Klansmen could close on them. Ambulances took the victims to a hospital. Angry whites soon surrounded the building.

In Birmingham, Fred Shuttlesworth, an African-American minister, got word of the riders' plight. He organized an auto caravan of deacons and ministers to go into Anniston and get the riders out.

The Trailways bus did not fare much better. It, too, was stopped at Anniston, by a group of men who beat the black riders in the front of the bus and forced them into the back. The bus made it to Birmingham, where yet another mob attacked the riders—this time with iron bars.

So it was that both teams ended up in Birmingham—battered, bloodied, and stunned by the attacks. None of them were in any condition to continue the ride. They decided to fly to New Orleans for the *Brown* anniversary observances.

SNCC stepped in to keep the rides going. Diane Nash rounded up volunteers from the Nashville group. As she later explained:

> If the Freedom Riders had been stopped as a result of violence, I strongly felt that the future of the Movement was going to be cut short. The impression would have been that whenever a movement starts, all [you have to do] is attack it with massive violence and the blacks [will] stop.[6]

The Freedom Rides continued all over the South. Riders were harassed, beaten, arrested, and thrown

This Greyhound bus was attacked by a mob of whites in Mississippi. The Freedom Riders barely escaped with their lives.

in jail. If one rider quit, another took his or her place. In that summer of 1961, over four hundred people, black and white, rode the Freedom Buses.

In November 1961, the Interstate Commerce Commission (ICC) banned segregation in transportation facilities. Unlike the Court, the ICC did not make rulings of law. It set regulations for the transportation industry. The ICC could impose fines or even revoke the licenses of companies that did not obey those regulations.

The Freedom Riders and the sit-in protesters always knew they were doing more than fighting for the right to eat a hamburger at Woolworth's or sit in the main waiting room at the Greyhound depot. They were building a foundation for freedom.

Risking their lives in the effort was part of the bargain, part of the commitment they had made. Jim Zwerg, a white Freedom Rider who was beaten nearly to death in Montgomery, summed up this commitment when he was interviewed in his hospital room:

> Segregation must be stopped. It must be broken down. Those of us on the Freedom Ride will continue. No matter what happens we are dedicated to this. We will take the beatings. We are willing to accept death. We are going to keep going until we can ride anywhere in the South.[7]

7

Activism in the Deep South

Peple in the civil rights movement—referred to by many as simply the Movement—expected to make sacrifices. For many of them, the fight for civil rights became not only a cause, but a way of life.

This was especially true in the five states of the Deep South: Alabama, Georgia, Louisiana, Mississippi, and South Carolina. Segregation was more deeply entrenched in these states than in the upper South. Race prejudice too often crossed over into race hatred, especially among poor whites in rural areas. African Americans were routinely terrorized. Civil rights workers from outside the region faced constant danger.

Braving Mississippi

SNCC well knew the perils of working in rural Mississippi. Still, they considered it necessary. They not only wanted to bring hope and help to the people, but they also wanted to show the federal government that something had to be done.

On the reason for going to Mississippi, the SNCC leadership agreed. But they could not agree on the best approach. The original Nashville group favored the nonviolent social action they had learned from Jim Lawson. They planned to use sit-ins, boycotts, and protest marches.

Another faction wanted to focus on political solutions. They believed that helping African Americans to vote would improve their political and economic situation and enable them to overturn Jim Crow laws.

The disagreement became so heated that it threatened to tear SNCC apart. Rather than allow that to happen, the two sides finally agreed to work on both goals at once.

Bob Moses, whose dedication had won the respect of both factions, would begin a voter education program in McComb. Marion Barry, who would one day become mayor of Washington, D.C., would arrive later to organize sit-ins. Others went to Jackson for community organizing. None succeeded as they had hoped.

Jim Bevel and Bernard Lafayette, who went to Jackson, were experienced community organizers and veterans of the Freedom Rides. These credentials did not take them very far in Jackson.

Adults and high school age young people did not want to listen. A lifetime of oppression had convinced them that the cause was hopeless. Bevel and Lafayette found themselves organizing a children's crusade. Thirteen- and fourteen-year-olds were still hopeful, still impressed to meet two real Freedom Riders.

With the unquestioning confidence of the young, they took chances that older people would not even consider. In the racial climate of Jackson, these young activists did not have to stage elaborate demonstrations. All they had to do was walk into the white section of the Greyhound depot to be arrested.

Their youth proved to be an advantage. White police who might have been rough on adults would not mistreat children. Some seemed more amused than anything else.

Police captain J. L. Ray eventually grew tired of seeing so many African-American youngsters coming through his jail. He warned the men to stop. Jim Bevel, whose dedication to the Movement sometimes led him to overlook the real consequences for real people, was determined to keep going: "[Captain Ray] can't tell me what to do and what not to do—I don't care if it is Mississippi or not," Bevel told Lafayette. "These children have a right to be free; they can make these decisions themselves."[1]

Lafayette tried to convince Bevel to back off; the children were too young, he said. They could not possibly realize the dangers of what they were doing.

Bevel, who was known for being rigid in his opinions, would not budge. Finally, both he and Lafayette were arrested for contributing to the delinquency of minors.

For two long weeks, police kept them in a large holding cell, without letting them shower or change clothes. In court, they came before a judge who was more interested in getting them out of town than throwing them in jail. He gave each defendant a $2,000 fine and a two-year suspended sentence. He warned that if they ever came before him again, they would not find him so generous.

Peaceful civil rights demonstrators were often treated brutally by police. Here a police dog attacks an African-American man during a protest outside the courthouse in Jackson, Mississippi.

In McComb, Bob Moses and his team encountered even more vicious resistance. The Ku Klux Klan regularly terrorized the black community, and the local authorities refused to help African-American victims. Bob Moses was brutally beaten while trying to register a small group of black voters.

His attacker, Billy Jack Caston, was the cousin of the sheriff and the son-in-law of E. H. Hurst, a member of the Mississippi State Legislature. Moses pressed charges, but Caston's trial became a sham. Moses explained:

> [Black witnesses] were advised not to sit in the courthouse except while we testified, otherwise we were in the back room. After we testified, the sheriff came back and told us that he didn't think it was safe for us to remain there while the jury gave its decision. . . . We read in the papers the next day that Billy Jack Caston had been acquitted.[2]

An even worse fate could await local African Americans who worked with Moses. Herbert Lee, a farmer with nine children, helped recruit black people to register for the vote. On September 25, 1961, state legislator E. H. Hurst shot him down in cold blood. An all-white jury quickly acquitted Hurst of the crime.

Bob Moses and his people were not surprised by the verdict. They had expected nothing else.

James Meredith and Ole Miss

The year 1961 saw the beginning of another civil rights landmark in the state of Mississippi. James Meredith applied for admission to the University of

Mississippi, or Ole Miss, as it is affectionately known. Though Meredith was qualified, the university turned him down.

It took a fifteen-month legal battle before the Fifth Judicial Circuit Court ordered Ole Miss to admit James Meredith. On September 30, 1962, federal marshals escorted Meredith to his dormitory. The campus erupted. An ever-growing mob tossed everything from bricks and bottles to homemade bombs at Meredith and the marshals. Some people began shooting. Marshals fell wounded, but they were under orders not to fire. All they could do was lob tear gas grenades into the crowd.

President John F. Kennedy sent in federal troops. Some thirty thousand soldiers arrived at Ole Miss, expecting to face a riot. It was more like a full-scale war.

Army veteran Ted Cowsert recalled the scene that greeted the troops that night on the campus:

> There was a lot of gasoline burning, a lot of automobiles burning on campus. Every concrete bench was broken, being thrown at us. I spent time in Vietnam. I'll take that any time over Ole Miss.[3]

The riots ended with two civilians dead, twenty-eight marshals wounded, and 160 others injured. On October 1, James Meredith attended his first class.

In spite of the ongoing danger, he stayed in school. His determination paid off. In 1964, he became the first African American in history to graduate from the University of Mississippi.

The Battle in Birmingham

In the spring of 1963, the Movement focused on Birmingham, Alabama. Many called it the most segregated city in the South, and for good reason. It had strict laws to separate the races, an openly racist police commissioner known as "Bull" Connor, and an active Ku Klux Klan.

Martin Luther King, Jr., and the SCLC knew that winning Birmingham would be a civil rights milestone. To them, that made it worth the risk.

The Birmingham plan, called Project C, for "confrontation," began on April 3, 1963. On that morning, some sixty-five people, both African American and white, gathered to receive their orders. While they got ready to march, the Reverend Fred Shuttlesworth worked behind the scenes.

Shuttlesworth, the minister whose daring rescue saved stranded Freedom Riders in 1961, wrote a "Birmingham Manifesto" and gave it to the press. It stated the grievances of the city's African Americans and the objectives they hoped to achieve.

Shuttlesworth also sent two of his people to Bull Connor's office to request a demonstration permit. True to form, Connor threw them out. "I will picket you over to the City Jail!" he bellowed.[4]

The demonstrators fully expected him to keep his word as they began sit-ins at five downtown stores. To their surprise, four of the stores simply closed their lunch counters when the demonstrators arrived. Only one called the police as Bull Connor had instructed.

Just twenty-one people went to jail that day. Martin Luther King, Jr., and his associates found themselves in an odd position—trying to figure out how to get more protesters arrested. Mass arrests made headlines and crowded the city jails. They turned breaking the law into a moral statement about injustice.

On April 6, the demonstrators tried a new tactic. Fred Shuttlesworth led about forty people in a protest march on City Hall. There in Bull Connor's own territory, they were promptly arrested.

The next day was Good Friday, one of the holiest days in the Christian year. Three African-American ministers observed it by leading another group of marchers to city hall, where they were also arrested.

After nine days, the demonstrations seemed stalled. They had not captured the interest of the press or the enthusiasm of Birmingham's African-American community. Martin Luther King, Jr., did two things: He sent for SNCC's Jim Bevel in Greenwood, Mississippi, and he personally led a march on city hall to get himself arrested. Bull Connor was only too happy to oblige.

Jim Bevel arrived in town on the day King went to jail. After his children's marches in Jackson, Mississippi, Bevel had a reputation for being both daring and imaginative. In Birmingham, he would prove that the reputation was well deserved.

The Children's Crusade

Bevel quickly decided that his Jackson tactics would work in Birmingham. He went to work recruiting, beginning with high school students and working his way down to younger children.

Organizing the young demonstrators was easier than convincing Martin Luther King, Jr., and the other Project C leaders to send a band of children out to face Bull Connor. They finally agreed. Bevel's idea was daring, but his reasoning made sense. He explained:

> Most adults have bills to pay—house notes, rents, car notes, utility bills . . . but the young people . . . are not hooked with all those responsibilities. A boy from high school has the same effect in terms of being in jail, in terms of putting pressure on the city, as his father, and yet there's no economic threat to the family, because the father is still on the job.[5]

On May 2, the children's crusade began. Around one o'clock, fifty teenagers marched downtown. They moved proudly, without hesitation, singing "We Shall Overcome." They were promptly arrested and put into patrol wagons.

Wave after wave of young marchers followed. So many marched that the police ran out of patrol wagons. They began loading children into school buses for the trip to jail. By the end of the day, every jail cell in Birmingham was crammed full of children.

The next morning, more than a thousand children marched. Bull Connor ordered out attack dogs and special fire hoses called monitor guns. They forced water from two high-powered hoses through a single nozzle. The resulting stream sent human bodies tumbling helplessly down the street.

Movement leaders realized that children's marches would be an effective form of protest. Here children are herded into jail following a demonstration in Birmingham in 1963.

Even that did not stop the marchers. Still they came. They crowded the downtown area yet boycotted all the stores. Because of the threat of violence from Bull Connor and his men, white people stayed out of town.

Civic leaders faced social and economic disaster. They decided that they had no choice but to negotiate with the demonstrators.

On May 10, 1963, Martin Luther King, Jr., Ralph Abernathy, and Fred Shuttlesworth faced television cameras and a crowd of impatient reporters. Shuttlesworth made a triumphant announcement: "Birmingham reached an accord with its conscience today. The acceptance of responsibility by local white and Negro leadership offers an example of a free people uniting to meet and solve their problems."[6]

The agreement contained the major points of Shuttlesworth's "Birmingham Manifesto": integrated rest rooms, lunch counters, and other facilities; jobs for African Americans in previously all-white occupations; and a biracial committee to oversee the integration process.

That night at St. John's Church, two thousand African Americans gathered to sing hymns and rejoice. The wisest among them knew that their struggles were not over. The likes of Bull Connor and the Ku Klux Klan would see to that.

Even the certainty of more hard days ahead could not spoil their joy. Against impossible odds, they had prevailed in the most segregated city of the Deep South. For the moment, that was cause enough for celebration.

To white segregationists, it was cause for alarm. If an army of black children could destroy the racial divide in Birmingham, then white supremacy was in danger everywhere.

8

"We Shall Overcome": The Movement Expands

The fallout from Birmingham brought a new urgency to the civil rights conflict. During the summer of 1963, African Americans marched, boycotted, and went to jail in record numbers. Segregationists dug in their heels and fought back with unrelenting fury.

In the first ten weeks of the summer, there were more than 750 demonstrations in 186 different cities. Nearly fifteen thousand people were arrested.[1]

Standing in the Schoolhouse Door

The first major post-Birmingham confrontation centered on the University of

85

Civil rights protesters were sometimes sprayed with monitor guns, high-pressure fire hoses strong enough to knock people down. Here marchers in Birmingham hold hands to stand against the force of the water.

Alabama. Two African-American students, Vivian Malone and James Hood, had won the right to enroll at 'Bama, as the University was nicknamed. They would follow in the steps of Autherine Lucy, who had won that right in 1956, only to have it snatched away by violence.

This time, things were different. Not even the grandstanding of newly elected governor George Wallace could stop integration at the university. During his campaign, Wallace had vowed to "[stand] at the schoolhouse door in person, if necessary" to prevent integration.[2] When Malone and Hood came to register for classes, he kept that vow.

On the morning of June 11, a federal motorcade pulled up in front of Foster Auditorium. George Wallace waited for them. He had even ordered his people to draw a chalk line across the floor. Its message was clear—"this far and no farther."

Assistant U.S. Attorney General Nicolas Katzenbach deliberately ignored that message. He crossed the line to hand the governor an order from President Kennedy. Then he asked if Wallace would obey it.

The governor said no and launched into an angry speech. He denounced the federal government and proclaimed a state's right to choose its own racial policies. Then he walked away.

The "show," as Katzenbach called it, ended for the moment. Behind the scenes there was frantic activity. Justice department officials smuggled Malone and Hood into the dormitories and got them set up in their rooms.

When Governor George Wallace returned to the schoolhouse door, he would not face Nicolas Katzenbach again. Instead, a small, federalized unit of the Alabama National Guard would confront the governor.

That afternoon, National Guard general Henry Graham faced Wallace with only four soldiers at his side. He saluted the governor and said, "Sir, it is my sad duty to ask you to step aside under orders from the President of the United States."[3]

Without further protest, the governor turned and walked away. The standoff was over. George Wallace's defiant gesture made him a hero to the white supremacists who had voted him into office.

The Assassination of Medgar Evers

Inspired by the historic Birmingham agreement, NAACP officer Medgar Evers asked for a biracial commission to plan the desegregation of Jackson, Mississippi. It was time for such a plan, he said. Birmingham had proved that; Birmingham had changed everything: "In the racial picture things will never be the same as they once were. History has reached a turning point, here and over the world."[4]

The mere thought of integration in Jackson enraged white supremacist Byron De La Beckwith. He believed that Medgar Evers had gone too far. On June 12, Beckwith lay in wait outside the Evers's home. When Evers appeared in the driveway, Beckwith shot him twice in the back.

Medgar Evers died in front of his wife and two small children, who came running out of the house. He was thirty-eight years old.

Byron De La Beckwith was tried twice for the crime, but both juries deadlocked without reaching a verdict. Not until February 5, 1994, was Beckwith finally convicted of the murder. Sentenced to a life term, he died in prison in January 2001. He was eighty years old.

On the day of Evers's funeral, some five thousand mourners held a silent march in his honor. When the grim procession arrived at the mortuary, family and close friends went inside for a small, private service.

As the crowd outside began breaking up, some of the young people formed a spontaneous march toward downtown. They were not experienced protesters, trained in the ways of nonviolence. They were grief-stricken, angry—and many of them were spoiling for a fight.

The marchers soon found themselves facing a line of police armed with shotguns. Firefighters backed them, with high-pressure hoses at the ready.

The marchers shouted angry slogans. Some of them began to hurl bricks at the police line. The situation had all the makings of a bloody riot until Justice Department official John Doar stepped into the middle of it.

Doar, who is white, was known as a defender of African-American civil rights. He had earned the respect of activists all over the South. He was able to calm the crowd and persuade them to leave.

Still, the narrow brush with violence worried Movement leaders. Nonviolence had been the mainstay of their demonstrations from the beginning. They wanted to keep it that way.

"I Have a Dream"

After the children's marches in Birmingham and the Medgar Evers assassination in Mississippi, President Kennedy sent a major civil rights bill to Congress. It not only banned segregation in public facilities, but it also called for an end to discrimination in employment. It established an Equal Employment Opportunity Commission to enforce fair employment practices.

The bill was so important that it brought the major civil rights groups together. Under the leadership of A. Philip Randolph, they gathered to plan what would become the largest protest demonstration in American history—the March for Jobs and Freedom.

For Randolph, the march fulfilled a lifelong dream. He had believed in mass action since the Pullman porters' strike. In 1941, the mere threat of a massive march on Washington had helped convince President Franklin D. Roosevelt to end racial discrimination in hiring for government and military jobs.

Twenty-two years later, on August 28, 1963, A. Philip Randolph led 250,000 demonstrators to the Lincoln Memorial. The power of nonviolence was never more dramatically displayed than on that day. A sea of humanity, black and white, packed together to listen, to sing, to give heartfelt shouts of "Amen!" and "Right on!" as a steady progression of speakers and performers made their appeal for civil rights.

Most of the speakers focused on the Deep South. But social worker Whitney Young struck a new note. As executive director of the National Urban League, he talked about the problems facing African Americans in the northern cities. It was an issue that would become increasingly important in the months and years ahead.

The Urban League was founded in 1910 to help southern African Americans find jobs when they moved to northern cities. Half a century later, the league was still coping with employment issues in the North.

Black people in the cities, Young said, might not have to fight Jim Crow. But they, too, had their battles:

> They must march from the rat infested, overcrowded ghettos to decent . . . residential areas. . . . They must march from the relief rolls to the established retraining centers. . . . They must march from the congested, ill-equipped schools which breed dropouts. . . . And finally, they must march from a present feeling of despair and hopelessness, despair and frustration, to renewed faith and confidence.[5]

The last speaker of the day was Martin Luther King, Jr. He talked about the way things were and the way they ought to be. He talked about freedom and justice. And he talked about a dream:

> I say to you today, my friends, that in spite of the difficulties and frustrations of the moment, I still have a dream. . . . I have a dream that one day this nation will rise up and live out the true meaning of its creed: "We hold these truths to be self-evident: that all men are created equal." . . . I have a dream that my four children will one day live in a nation where they will not be judged by the color of their skin but by the content of their character.[6]

He ended with a rousing call to

> let freedom ring. . . . When we let freedom ring, when we let it ring from every village and every hamlet, from every state and every city, we will be able to speed up that day when all of God's children, black men and white men, Jews and

At the 1963 March on Washington, Martin Luther King, Jr., and other speakers addressed a crowd of over two hundred thousand, while millions more watched on television.

Gentiles, Protestants and Catholics, will be able to join hands and sing in the words of the old Negro spiritual, "Free at last! free at last! thank God Almighty, we are free at last![7]

When King had finished, thousands joined to sing "We Shall Overcome." Television brought the scene into millions of American homes. It was a moment that the nation would never forget.

Four Little Girls

Just eighteen days after the march on Washington, on September 15, 1963, a bomb exploded at the Sixteenth Street Baptist Church in Birmingham, Alabama. The bombers timed the explosion for maximum damage: Sunday at 10:22 A.M., when the church was filled with worshipers.

According to the Reverend John Cross, the blast sounded

> like the whole world was shaking. All around me was so much dust and soot—and glass had fallen, and plaster from the walls and ceiling . . . and it was so smoky in there that some of the people could hardly be identifiable three feet away from me.[8]

When rescuers picked through the rubble they found the bodies of four little girls: Addie Mae Collins, Carole Robertson, and Cynthia Wesley, all fourteen years old, and Denise McNair, who was two months shy of her twelfth birthday.

About two thousand African Americans gathered outside the church. Some roamed the streets, hurling rocks and bottles at white motorists. Here and there, gunshots rang out. Gunfire killed two African-American teenagers and injured a third. Downtown Birmingham looked like a war zone.

Federal Bureau of Investigation (FBI) agents traced the crime to four Ku Klux Klan members, but did not bring charges against them. FBI director J. Edgar Hoover decided not to prosecute, claiming that no Alabama jury would ever convict the men.

Fourteen years later, in 1977, conditions had changed. Alabama Attorney General Bill Baxley built a case against Robert Chambliss—a Ku Klux Klan member known as "Dynamite Bob." An Alabama jury found Chambliss guilty of first-degree murder in the church bombing, and an Alabama judge sentenced him to life in prison. Chambliss lived the last seven years of his life in a prison cell, dying on October 19, 1985.

Four little girls—Denise McNair, Carole Robertson, Addie Mae Collins, and Cynthia Wesley—died when a bomb ripped through the Sixteenth Street Baptist Church. The bombers were members of the Ku Klux Klan. One died without being charged; the other three were found guilty and imprisoned many years later.

The other three suspects escaped prosecution at that time, largely because Bill Baxley's term as attorney general came to an end. One of them, Herman Frank Cash, died of natural causes in 1994. The FBI eventually brought charges against the other two. On May 1, 2001, Thomas Blanton, Jr., was sentenced to life in prison. Just over a year later, on May 22, 2002, the conviction of Bobby Frank Cherry finally brought closure to a case that had spanned thirty-nine years.

Like the 1955 murder of fourteen-year-old Emmett Till, the Sixteenth Street Baptist Church bombing became a turning point for the Movement. The sheer brutality of it shocked the nation, as TV newscaster Walter Cronkite explained:

> I don't think the white community really understood the depths of the problem and the depths of the hate of the Klan and its friends in the South, and in the North too for that matter, until . . . the bomb went off and those four little girls were blasted and buried in the debris of the church. . . . This was the awakening.[9]

The Civil Rights Act of 1964

The Sixteenth Street bombing prompted Congress to pass President Kennedy's civil rights bill over the objections of southern members. Sadly, Kennedy was not alive to sign it. He had been assassinated on November 22, 1963, just five weeks after Addie Mae Collins, Carole Robertson, Cynthia Wesley, and Denise McNair died in the rubble of Sixteenth Street Baptist Church.

President Lyndon B. Johnson signed the Civil

Rights Act of 1964 into law on July 2. It was the most sweeping piece of civil rights legislation since the end of reconstruction.

The act prohibited discrimination based on "race, color, religion, or national origin"[10] in all public accommodations. This meant everything from water fountains and restrooms to restaurants, hotels, and hospitals. Special sections dealt with discrimination in public schools, federally funded programs, and employment.

The new law dismantled the Jim Crow system, forcing the South to begin a process of change. Hardcore white supremacists frantically looked for loopholes. They found one that focused on voting rights. The Civil Rights Act allowed restrictions such as residency requirements and literacy tests. The segregationists used those restrictions to keep African Americans from voting and slow the process of integration to a crawl.

9

The Turn to Militancy

Beginning in the summer of 1964, both sides in the civil rights struggle focused on voting rights. Movement leaders planned massive voter registration drives. White supremacists fought to prevent blacks from exercising this basic right of citizenship.

This conflict would produce two of the civil rights movement's most storied operations: the 1964 "Freedom Summer" in Mississippi and the 1965 Selma-to-Montgomery march in Alabama. They came at a time of a growing militancy in the African-American community.

Some African Americans were losing

97

faith in the principles of nonviolence. They wanted to strike out—to take what should be theirs, by force if necessary.

Malcolm X, Black Nationalism, and the Nation of Islam

Malcolm X was born Malcolm Little, but after converting to Islam, he rejected what he thought of as his "slave name" (because slaves were called by their masters' last names). He took the last name "X" to refer to the unknown name of his African ancestors.

At the beginning of his public career, Malcolm X wanted neither nonviolence nor integration. As a black nationalist and member of the Nation of Islam, he believed in meeting force with force. He accepted Black Muslim leader Elijah Muhammad's characterization of white people as "devils" and wanted nothing to do with them. His goal was a separate black nation, built on land to be donated by the U.S. government.

He did not consider this donation as charity. It would be payment for the years of slavery endured by African Americans.

A fiery speaker who did not fear controversy, Malcolm X became Elijah Muhammad's chief deputy. In time, he began to think beyond Muhammad's teachings. He decided that white people might not be devils after all and that some cooperation between the races—and indeed, among people of all races—might be possible.

In 1964, his changing views led him to split with

the Nation of Islam. That summer, he formed the Organization of Afro-American Unity (OAAU). It called for racial pride, armed self-defense, and the creation of black-run businesses and institutions. It did not call for violence against whites or for a separate black nation.

The break with Elijah Muhammad was bitter on both sides. On February 21, 1965, it turned deadly. Malcolm planned to present the OAAU program to a large group at the Audubon Ballroom in New York City. He had just taken the stage when three members of the Nation of Islam rushed forward and shot him dead.

The OAAU did not survive the death of Malcolm X, and black nationalism was never quite the same. When Elijah Muhammad died in 1975, his son Wallace took over.

Wallace Muhammad softened the Nation's message, brought it more into line with traditional Islam, and even opened membership to people of all races. He also changed the name of the organization, first to World Community of Islam in the West and later to the American Muslim Mission.

The new focus caused a split in the group. In 1977, Louis Farrakhan formed a new Nation of Islam, based upon the teachings of Elijah Muhammad.

The Mississippi Freedom Summer

In 1964, while Malcolm X and the Nation of Islam preached black nationalism and hatred of whites,

Malcolm X was one of the black leaders who exemplified the new militancy. After breaking off from the Nation of Islam, he formed the Organization of Afro-American Unity. He was assassinated in 1965.

traditional, nonviolent activists operated the Freedom Summer project. CORE, SNCC, and the NAACP joined together to launch a massive voter registration drive in the Deep South. They started in Mississippi, because only 6.7 percent of its African-American citizens were registered to vote. That was the lowest percentage of any state in the nation.

In addition to voter registration, the activists established thirty "Freedom Schools" around the state. More than three thousand black children came to these schools to study subjects like civics, African-American history, and the philosophy of the civil rights movement.

The adults learned about participatory democracy by helping to organize a new political party, the Mississippi Freedom Democratic Party (MFDP). The MFDP drew up a party platform, or statement of principles. It also elected delegates to the Democratic National Convention in Atlantic City, New Jersey.

At this convention, the Democratic Party would choose its nominee for president. Most people expected Lyndon B. Johnson to win handily. He had stepped into the presidency after the Kennedy assassination. Now he would stand for election in his own right.

Political conventions can be boring when there is little or no question about the presidential nominee. This convention would not be boring; the MFDP would see to that.

The party challenged the official Mississippi delegation for the right to represent their state at the convention. Though the challenge failed, civil rights activist Fannie Lou Hamer transformed that failure into a kind of victory. She stopped the convention in its tracks by leading MFDP delegates in singing freedom songs from the floor of the convention.

She also made a speech, explaining the personal and social cost of voter registration work. Many were arrested and beaten. Hamer remembered her own experiences in jail:

> [The police] beat me with the long flat blackjack. I screamed to God in pain. . . . All of this on account we want to register, to become first-class citizens, and if the Freedom Democratic party is not seated now, I question America.[1]

Mississippi Burning

The MFDP challenge came just twenty days after a grisly discovery in Mississippi. On August 4, FBI investigators had found the bodies of three missing civil rights workers—two whites and one black.

Andrew Goodman, Michael Schwerner, and James Chaney had disappeared on June 21, while driving between the towns of Longview and Meridian. Sheriff's deputy Cecil Price stopped their car, supposedly for a traffic violation.

They were questioned and briefly jailed, then allowed to leave. Back on the road, Klansmen pursued and stopped their car. They shot the three men and dumped their bodies into an earthen dam. Weeks of searching had turned up nothing. Then a Klansman told the FBI where to look.

Investigators identified nineteen men who took

part in the murders, including Deputy Price and Sheriff Lawrence Rainey. Justice Department attorney John Doar knew that no Mississippi court would convict them of murder.

He decided to take a different route, charging all nineteen with violating the civil rights of the victims. This made the killings a federal crime.

The Mississippi Burning trial, as it came to be called after the FBI code name, began on October 7,

MISSING CALL FBI

THE FBI IS SEEKING INFORMATION CONCERNING THE DISAPPEARANCE AT PHILADELPHIA, MISSISSIPPI, OF THESE THREE INDIVIDUALS ON JUNE 21, 1964. EXTENSIVE INVESTIGATION IS BEING CONDUCTED TO LOCATE GOODMAN, CHANEY, AND SCHWERNER, WHO ARE DESCRIBED AS FOLLOWS:

ANDREW GOODMAN   JAMES EARL CHANEY   MICHAEL HENRY SCHWERNER

Andrew Goodman, James Chaney, and Michael Schwerner were three civil rights workers who disappeared during their efforts to register black voters in Mississippi. They had been killed by racists, including a sheriff and deputy.

1967. John Doar and his Justice Department legal team faced an all-white jury and a judge who favored segregation. In spite of this, Doar got guilty verdicts against seven of the killers. It was the first time in Mississippi history that a jury had convicted white defendants of civil rights crimes. The men were sentenced to federal prison for terms ranging from three to ten years.

The Struggle in Selma

In the spring of 1965, yet another landmark confrontation centered around African-American voting rights. In January, Martin Luther King, Jr., came to Selma, Alabama, to announce "the beginning of a determined, organized, mobilized campaign to get the right to vote everywhere in Alabama."[2]

Selma was a town of some 30,000 people, located in Dallas County. More than 15,000 African Americans lived in the county; only 156 of them were registered to vote.

Selma's sheriff, Jim Clark, was known for his vicious responses to black protest. A picture of him wielding a club as he pushed schoolteacher Amelia Boynton to the ground made major newspapers all over the country. When Clark arrested Boynton, a hundred Selma teachers marched on the courthouse in protest.

In nearby Marion, police and state troopers attacked a peaceful group of demonstrators. Vietnam veteran Jimmie Lee Jackson was shot in the stomach. He died seven days later.

Jim Bevel helped to organize a funeral march that was at once a tribute to Jackson and a protest against the racism that took his life. After the service, Bevel and others began planning a more ambitious march: from Selma to the state capitol in Montgomery, fifty-four miles away.

Marching to Montgomery

On Sunday, March 7, six hundred people set out on what was to be a five-day pilgrimage. They never made it out of Selma. At a bridge on the edge of town, police and state troopers met them with tear gas and billy clubs. Governor George Wallace had ordered the officers to stop the march by any means necessary.

The officers shouted a warning. Moments later, they attacked the unarmed marchers. The melee made the evening news on TV stations all over the country.

Millions watched in horror as the scene unfolded on their screens. One viewer remembered the moment when the police waded into the crowd of marchers:

> A shrill cry of terror . . . rose up as the troopers lumbered forward, stumbling sometimes on the fallen bodies. . . . the top of a helmeted head [would emerge] from the cloud [of gas], followed by a club on the upswing. . . . *Unhuman.* No other word can describe the motions.[3]

Martin Luther King, Jr., rushed to Selma and helped to organize another march, this one scheduled for Tuesday. To avoid more violence, King asked for a court order against police interference. When the order did not come through, the protesters settled for a symbolic march. They went to the bridge but did not cross over. Instead, they held a prayer vigil, then turned around and went home.

Finally, a federal judge ruled that the state could not interfere with the marchers. President Johnson put the Alabama National Guard under federal control to enforce the ruling.

On March 21, the protesters again set out from Selma. This time they crossed the bridge and kept going. Five days later they arrived in Montgomery; twenty-five thousand strong and jubilant at their success.

The Selma march helped to push the Voting Rights Act of 1965 through Congress. President Johnson signed it into law on August 6. It abolished voter eligibility tests that could be used to discriminate against African Americans. It also allowed federal supervision of voter registration and elections in counties that had used eligibility tests. If necessary, federal examiners could replace local registrars to ensure fairness.

Within a few months, more than 250,000 new African-American voters had registered. Together with the Civil Rights Act of 1964, the Voting Rights Act of 1965 transformed racial policy in the South. These two laws were the crowning achievements of the Movement that began ten years earlier, with the Supreme Court decision in *Brown* v. *Board of Education of Topeka*.

The Watts Riots

The activists had little time to celebrate. Just five days after President Johnson signed the Voting Rights Act, a routine traffic stop transformed a black ghetto in Los Angeles, California, into a war zone.

The neighborhood known as Watts was in the middle of a heat wave on that August 11. When a white policeman pulled over a young black motorist, a fight broke out and soon turned into a full-scale race riot. For five days, African-American mobs raged through the streets, burning and looting. By the time the violence ended, thirty-four people were dead and more than a thousand wounded. Estimates put property damage at $45 million.

Watts was a terrifying wake-up call for America. Instead of Jim Crow in the rural South, African Americans began to focus on the brutalizing poverty and hopelessness of the urban ghettos, or poor black neighborhoods. A new generation of leaders in CORE and SNCC turned away from the philosophy of nonviolence.

Black Power

The militant Stokely Carmichael became president of SNCC in May 1966. He soon turned it into a center for the growing Black Power movement.

Black Power advocates called for racial and cultural pride, economic and social independence from whites, and armed self-defense. Stokely Carmichael summed it up as "a call for black people in this country to unite, to recognize their heritage, and to build a sense of community."[4]

The next SNCC president, H. Rap Brown, changed the organization's name: The "N" no longer stood for "Nonviolent," but for "National." To Brown, white America was the enemy. When the summer of 1967 brought race riots in 164 cities around the country, he praised the violence and called for more.

Perhaps the best known of the Black Power groups was the Black Panther Party. Formed in Oakland, California, by college students Huey P. Newton and Bobby Seale, it had a paramilitary, or military-like, style. The Panthers wore combat fatigues and black berets and considered themselves a defense force for the oppressed.

Members of the militant groups were defiant. They were black. They were proud. "Black is beautiful" they said, and they showed their pride with enormous "Afro" hairdos and colorful ceremonial robes. They symbolized Black Power as the restrained, suit-and-tie marchers of the fifties and early sixties symbolized integration.

Black militancy did not set well with many white Americans, who feared and distrusted it. The Movement as a whole lost so much support that President Johnson's 1966 Civil Rights Bill failed to pass Congress. Not even Martin Luther King, Jr., could stem the tide. His attempt to organize antipoverty marches in Chicago in 1967 met with lukewarm results.

Increasingly, white activists turned their attention from civil rights to the war in Vietnam. Many

African Americans also denounced United States military involvement in that small, Southeast Asian nation. Activists of all races called upon young men to resist the draft and refuse to serve in the military.

The antiwar movement used the nonviolent strategies pioneered by the early civil rights activists. So too did other groups with a cause. For example, the Mexican American, Native American, and women's movements made important advances in the late sixties and early seventies.

In the midst of this shifting focus, an assassin shot and killed Martin Luther King, Jr. It happened on April 4, 1968, in Memphis, Tennessee.

King's death represented the end of an era. For many, Martin Luther King, Jr., *was* the Movement, or at least its heart and soul. He had continued to preach Christian nonviolence, even as more militant activists discarded it.

A Summing Up

Neither Martin Luther King, Jr., nor any other activist managed to end racism or create a color-blind society. However, the Movement did accomplish many things. It overturned *Plessy* v. *Ferguson*, ended legal segregation in the public schools, and dismantled Jim Crow segregation in the South.

From lunch counters and bus depots to voting booths and workplaces, the Movement established a new reality for African Americans. Once, racial segregation was the norm in the South. White people enforced it because many of them considered blacks

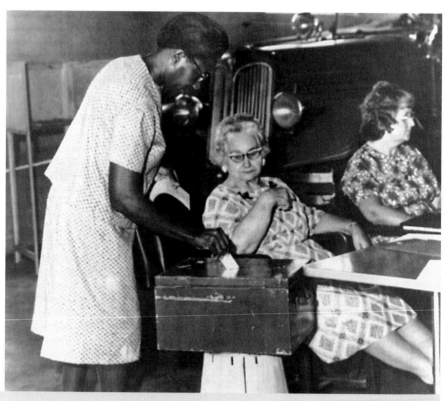

An African-American woman votes in a congressional primary election in Mississippi in 1967. Achieving voting rights for blacks was one of the greatest achievements of the civil rights movement.

inferior. Black people accepted it because they saw no other choice. Then along came the Movement to challenge white America's racial ideas.

With marches and sit-ins and acts of civil disobedience, it focused public attention on the injustice of racism and segregation. It gave black Americans hope for a better future and served notice on the white power structure that things had to change.

And things did change. In 1976, Central High School in Little Rock, Arkansas elected its first African-American student body president: Lloyd Myers, Jr. In 1996, former Alabama governor George Wallace apologized for his "stand in the schoolhouse door" to block integration at the University of Alabama.

Racial hatred still exists. The Ku Klux Klan and other white supremacist groups are still active in many parts of the country.

Bleak ghettos still trap thousands of African Americans in poverty. But one important thing is different: Racial segregation is against the law and no longer seems "normal" to most Americans. People of all races have become more aware of minority rights. These changes are the legacy of the civil rights movement of the fifties and sixties.

Chronology

1877—End of Reconstruction.

May 18, 1896—Supreme Court ruling in *Plessy* v. *Ferguson* establishes separate-but-equal doctrine.

February 12, 1909—NAACP founded.

1910—Urban League founded.

June 21, 1915—Grandfather clauses to exempt white voters from literacy tests declared unconstitutional.

September 17, 1919—Marcus Garvey's Black Star shipping line buys its first cargo ship.

August 25, 1925—Brotherhood of Sleeping Car Porters founded.

1930—Nation of Islam founded.

August 25, 1937—Brotherhood of Sleeping Car Porters signs a labor contract with the Pullman Company.

1942— Congress of Racial Equality (CORE) founded.

June 5, 1950—Supreme Court orders Herman Sweatt admitted to University of Texas Law School.

May 17, 1954—Supreme Court decides for plaintiffs in *Brown* v. *Board of Education of Topeka,* overthrowing the "separate but equal" doctrine of *Plessy* v. *Ferguson*.

December 1, 1955—Rosa Parks arrested for refusing to give up her bus seat to a white man.

February 3, 1956—Autherine Lucy enrolls in the University of Alabama School of Library Science.

March 12, 1956—Congressional representatives from eleven states sign the "Southern Manifesto."

November 13, 1956—Supreme Court strikes down bus segregation laws as unconstitutional.

1957—Southern Christian Leadership Council (SCLC) founded.

September 4, 1957—Little Rock Nine make first attempt to enter Central High School.

June 18, 1959—Arkansas school-closing law ruled unconstitutional.

February 1, 1960—Greensboro Four hold first lunch counter sit-in.

July 25, 1960—First black customer served at Woolworth's lunch counter in Greensboro.

October 1, 1962—James Meredith enters University of Mississippi, protected by federal marshals.

April 3, 1963—The Birmingham marches begin.

June 11, 1963—Alabama governor George Wallace makes his "stand in the schoolhouse door" to protest integration of the University of Alabama.

August 28, 1963—March on Washington brings 250,000 demonstrators to the nation's capital.

September 15, 1963—Bombing of Sixteenth Street Baptist Church in Birmingham kills four little girls.

November 22, 1963—President John F. Kennedy assassinated.

June 21, 1964—Three civil rights workers killed in Mississippi.

July 2, 1964—President Lyndon B. Johnson signs the Civil Rights Act of 1964 into law.

February 21, 1965—Malcolm X assassinated.

March 7, 1965—First Selma march ends in violence.

March 21, 1965—Marchers leave Selma, protected by troops. Five days later, they arrive in Montgomery.

August 6, 1965—President Johnson signs the Voting Rights Act of 1965 into law.

August 11, 1965—Watts riots begin.

1966—Black Panthers founded.

May 8, 1966—Stokely Carmichael elected president of SNCC.

October 7, 1967—Mississippi Burning trial begins.

April 4, 1968—Martin Luther King, Jr., assassinated.

Chapter Notes

Chapter 1. Slavery and Reconstruction

1. "Barbara Jordan (1936–1996). A Tribute," n.d., <www.elf.net/bjordan/> (September 2, 2002).

2. Roy P. Basler, ed., *The Collected Works of Abraham Lincoln*, Volume III, "Fourth Debate with Stephen A. Douglas at Charleston, Illinois" (September 18, 1858) (New Brunswick, N.J.: Rutgers University Press, 1953), pp. 145–146.

3. "The Civil Rights Act of March 1, 1875," excerpted from U.S. Statutes at Large, vol. XVIII, p. 335 ff., n.d., <http://chnm.gmu.edu/courses/122/recon/civilrightsact.html> (September 16, 2002).

4. "Eyewitness to Jim Crow: Edgar Williams Remembers" in *The History of Jim Crow*, n.d., <http://www.jimcrowhistory.org/resources/narratives/Edgar_Williams.htm> (September 15, 2002).

5. Leon F. Litwack, *Trouble in Mind: Black Southerners in the Age of Jim Crow* (New York: Alfred A. Knopf, 1998), p. 37.

6. Booker T. Washington. "The Road to Negro Progress," in *The Annals of America*, vol. 12 (London, England: Encyclopedia Britannica, Inc., 1976), pp. 10–11.

7. Ibid.

8. W.E.B. Du Bois, *The Souls of Black Folk: Of Our Spiritual Strivings*, n.d., <http://www.knowledgerush.com/paginated/soulb10/soulb10_s2_p2_pages.html> (October 2, 2003).

9. Ibid.

10. "Principles of the Niagara Movement," in *The Annals of America*, vol. 13 (London, England: Encyclopedia Britannica, Inc., 1976), p. 28.

Chapter 2. Beginnings of the Movement

1. Kwame Anthony Appiah and Henry Louis Gates, Jr., eds., *Africana: The Encyclopedia of the African and African American Experience* (New York: Basic Civitas Books, 1999), p. 871.

2. Sidney Bechet, *Treat It Gentle: An Autobiography* (New York: Da Capo Press, 2002), p. 96.

3. Appiah and Gates, p. 871.

4. "UNIA Declaration of Rights of the Negro Peoples of the World," New York, August 13, 1920, reprinted in Robert Hill, ed., *The Marcus Garvey and Universal Negro Improvement Papers*, vol. 2 (Berkeley: University of California Press, 1983), excerpted by *History Matters*, n.d., <http://historymatters.gmu.edu/d/5122> (September 25, 2002).

5. "Marcus Garvey Timeline," *American Experience*, n.d., <http://www.pbs.org/wgbh/amex/garvey/timeline/timeline2.html> (October 3, 2002).

6. "A. Philip Randolph: For Jobs and Freedom," *PBS.org*, n.d., <http://www.pbs.org/weta/apr/quotes.html> (September 15, 2002).

7. Edward Berman, "The Pullman Porters Win," *The Nation*, August 21, 1935, <http://newdeal.feri.org/nation/na35217.htm> (May 27, 2003).

8. David McCullough, *Truman* (New York: Simon and Schuster, 1992), p. 588.

Chapter 3. Challenging Jim Crow Segregation

1. "*Sweatt v. Painter Archival and Textural Resources*: U.S. Supreme Court Opinion," June 5, 1950, <http://www.law.du.edu/russell/lh/sweatt/docs/sweatt_ussc.html> (October 1, 2002).

2. Ed Cray, *Chief Justice: A Biography of Earl Warren* (New York: Simon and Schuster, 1997), p. 524.

3. Supreme Court of the United States, *Brown v. Board of Education*, 347 U.S. 483 (1954) (USSC+), The National Center for Public Policy Research, n.d.,

<http://www.nationalcenter.org/brown.html> (October 8, 2002).

4. David Halberstam, *The Fifties* (New York: Villard Books, 1993), p. 436.

Chapter 4. Montgomery, Alabama: The Bus Boycott

1. Taylor Branch, *Parting the Waters: America in the King Years 1954–1963* (New York: Simon and Schuster, Inc., 1988), p. 131.

2. Ibid., p. 133.

3. Clayborn Carson et al., eds., *The Papers of Martin Luther King, Jr., Volume 3: Birth of a New Age, December 1955–December 1956*, Martin Luther King, Jr., Papers Project at Stanford University, 2002, <http://www.stanford.edu/group/King/publications/speeches/MIA_mass_meeting> (October 15, 2002).

4. "Boycott: Before There Was a Dream There Was Montgomery," *inTime*, 2001, <http://www.time.com/time/teach/boycott/images/mag.pdf> (October 15, 2002)

5. "Fred Gray: Background," n.d., <http://www.fredgray.net/background.html> (October 13, 2002).

6. "Declaration of Southern Congressmen on Integration of Schools," in *The Annals of America*, vol. 17 (London, England: Encyclopedia Britannica, Inc., 1976), p. 372.

7. "Southern Christian Leadership Conference," Martin Luther King, Jr., Papers Project at Stanford University, 2002, <http://www.stanford.edu/group/King/about_king/encyclopedia/enc_SCLC. htm> (June 3, 2003).

8. Ibid.

Chapter 5. Pioneers in School Integration

1. *The Columbia World of Quotations*, Bartleby.com, 1996, <http://www.bartleby.com/66/14/37014.html> (October 31, 2003).

2. "Little Rock," *Spartacus Educational*, n.d.,

<http://www.spartacus.schoolnet.co.uk/USAlittle rock.htm> (October 17, 2002).

3. Ibid.

4. Dwight D. Eisenhower, "The Little Rock School Crisis," in *The Annals of America*, vol. 17 (London, England: Encyclopedia Britannica, Inc., 1976), p. 457.

5. Ibid, pp. 459–460.

6. "Understanding the Nine: Inside Central High 1957," *About.com*, n.d.,<http://littlerock.about.com/library/weekly/aa071300a.htm> (October 20, 2002).

7. Jack Schnedler, "What Happened After Central High Crisis?" *Arkansas-Democrat Gazette*, 1997, <http://www.ardemgaz.com/prev/central/wcentral 04.html> (October 20, 2002).

8. "Little Rock."

Chapter 6. The Beginnings of Sixties Activism

1. Jim Schlosser, "The Story of the Greensboro Sit-ins," n.d., <http://www.sitins.com> (October 26, 2002).

2. Taylor Branch, *Parting the Waters: America in the King Years 1954–1963* (New York: Simon and Schuster, Inc., 1988), p. 279.

3. "Thoughts," *Robert Moses Archives*, n.d., <http://216.247.70.125/vclass/seevak/groups/2001/sites/moses/archives/thoughts.htm> (October 22, 2002).

4. Juan Williams, *Eyes on the Prize: America's Civil Rights Years, 1954–1965* (New York: Viking Penguin Inc., 1987), p. 147.

5. Ibid.

6. Ibid., p. 149.

7. "Freedom Riders," *Spartacus Educational*, n.d., <http://www.spartacus.schoolnet.co.uk/USA freedomR.htm> (October 28, 2002).

Chapter 7. Activism in the Deep South

1. David Halberstam, *The Children* (New York: Random House, 1998), p. 393.

2. Robert Moses, "Mississippi: 1961–1962," in Clayborne Carson, David J. Garrow, Gerald Gill, Vincent Harding, and Darlene Clark Hine, eds., *The Eyes on the Prize Civil Rights Reader: Documents, Speeches, and Firsthand Accounts from the Black Freedom Struggle, 1954–1990* (New York: Penguin, 1991), pp. 170–175.

3. "Mississippi and Meredith Remember," *CNN.com*, October 1, 2002, <http://www.cnn.com/2002/US/South/09/30/meredith> (October 31, 2002).

4. Taylor Branch, Parting the Waters: America in the King Years 1954–1963 (New York: Simon and Schuster, Inc., 1988), p. 708.

5. Steven Kasher, *The Civil Rights Movement: A Photographic History, 1954–1968* (New York: Abeville Press, 1996), p. 94.

6. Diane McWhorter, *Carry Me Home: Birmingham, Alabama—The Climactic Battle of the Civil Rights Revolution* (New York: Simon and Schuster, 2001), p. 422.

Chapter 8. "We Shall Overcome": The Movement Expands

1. Taylor Branch, *Parting the Waters: America in the King Years 1954–1963* (New York: Simon and Schuster, Inc., 1988), p. 825.

2. Ibid.

3. Diane McWhorter, *Carry Me Home: Birmingham, Alabama—The Climactic Battle of the Civil Rights Revolution* (New York: Simon and Schuster, 2001), p. 462.

4. Ibid., p. 464.

5. Steven Kasher, *The Civil Rights Movement: A Photographic History, 1954–1968* (New York: Abeville Press, 1996), pp. 119–120.

6. Martin Luther King, Jr., "I Have a Dream," *University of Minnesota Human Rights Library*,

<http://www1.umn.edu/humanrts/education/luther speech.html> (September 25, 2003).

7. Ibid.

8. Greg Barber, "The Birmingham Church Bombing," *Online NewsHour*, n.d., <http://www.pbs. org/newshour/media/clarion/kc_birmingham.html> (November 16, 2002).

9. Jeff Hansen and John Archibald, "Church bomb felt like 'world shaking,'" *In the Memory of Four Little Girls*, September 15, 1997, <http://www.useekufind. com/peace/bombworldshaking.htm> (October 2, 2003).

10. Legal Information Institute, *US Code Collection*, Title 42, Chapter 21, Subchapter II, Sec. 200a-1, n.d., <http://www4.law.cornell.edu/uscode/42/2000a. html> (November 23, 2002).

Chapter 9. The Turn to Militancy

1. Milton Viorst, *Fire in the Streets: America in the 1960s* (New York: Simon and Schuster, 1979), p. 263.

2. "Violence in Selma 1965," *History Central*, n.d., <http://www.multied.com/Sixties/Selma.html> (November 25, 2002).

3. Steven Kasher, *The Civil Rights Movement: A Photographic History, 1954–1968* (New York: Abeville Press, 1996), p. 168.

4. "Black Power," *Spartacus Educational*, n.d., <http://www.spartacus.schoolnet.co.uk/USAblack power.htm> (June 5, 2003).

Glossary

alliance—A close association of groups with common interests.

Black Panthers—Group founded in 1966 by Huey P. Newton and Bobby Seale, who called for armed self-defense and African-American pride.

Black Power—A call for racial pride and African-American independence from white political, economic, and social institutions.

boycott—Banding together to refuse to patronize a particular business; a means of bringing economic pressure.

Brotherhood of Sleeping Car Porters (BSCP)—Group founded in 1925 as a labor union for African-American porters employed by the Pullman company.

Congress of Racial Equality (CORE)—Group founded in 1942 by college students in Chicago; used nonviolent means of protest, such as sit-ins and marches to bring about social change.

discrimination—Treatment based on class or category rather than individual merit.

emancipate—To free from bondage; liberate.

illiterate—Unable to read.

injunction—A court order prohibiting a particular course of action.

integration—Bringing people of different racial

groups into equal association; opposite of *segregation*.

Jim Crow—Name given to southern segregation laws; apparently based upon a minstrel show character.

Ku Klux Klan—A white racist organization that originated after the Civil War.

labor union—An organization of workers formed to improve wages or working conditions for the whole membership.

National Association for the Advancement of Colored People (NAACP)—Group founded in 1909 by W.E.B. Du Bois and others; emphasized legal and political solutions for African-American problems.

Nation of Islam (Black Muslims)—Group founded in 1930 by Wallace Fard; practiced the Muslim religion and advocated black power.

Organization of Afro-American Unity (OAAU)—Black nationalist organization founded by Malcolm X in 1964.

prejudice—An opinion formed beforehand, without knowledge of the facts.

prosecute—To bring legal action against.

racism—The belief that one race is superior to others; discrimination or prejudice based on race.

servile—Submissive and self-deprecating.

sharecropper—A farmer who gives a share (usually half or more) of the crop to the landowner.

Southern Christian Leadership Conference (SCLC)—Group founded in 1957 by Martin Luther King, Jr., and others; advocated Christian Nonviolence.

stereotype—An oversimplified concept or image that takes no account of individual differences.

Student Nonviolent Coordinating Committee (SNCC)—Group founded in 1960 by a group of college students; advocated nonviolent social protest.

subordinate—Belonging to a lower or inferior class or rank.

tangible—Possible to touch; real or concrete.

Universal Negro Improvement Association (UNIA)—Black nationalist organization founded by Marcus Garvey in 1914.

urban—Characteristic of the city or city life.

Urban League—Group founded in 1910 to help African Americans from the South find jobs in Northern cities.

Further Reading

Bridges, Ruby, and Margo Lundell. *Through My Eyes*. New York: Scholastic, Inc., 1999.

Feinstein, Stephen. *The 1960s From the Vietnam War to Flower Power*. Berkeley Heights, N.J.: Enslow Publishers, Inc., 2000.

King, Casey, Linda Barret Osborne, and Joe Brooks. *Oh, Freedom!: Kids Talk About the Civil Rights Movement With the People Who Made It Happen*. New York: Knopf Publishing, 1997.

Levine, Ellen. *Freedom's Children: Young Civil Rights Activists Tell Their Own Stories*. New York: Puffin Books, 2000.

Polakow, Amy. *Daisy Bates: Civil Rights Crusader*. North Haven, Conn.: Linnet Books, 2003.

Tillage, Leon Walter, and Susan L. Roth. *Leon's Story*. Gordonsville, Va.: VHPS Holtzbrinck Publisher, 2000.

Wukovits, John F. *Martin Luther King, Jr*. San Diego, Calif.: Lucent Books, 1999.

Internet Addresses

"African American Odyssey" Library of Congress
<http://memory.loc.gov/ammem/aaohtml/exhibit/aointro.html>

Historic Places of the Civil Rights Movement
<http://www.cr.nps.gov/nr/travel/civilrights/>

National Civil Rights Museum
<http://www.mecca.org/~crights/cyber.html>

Index